NEW ORLEANS

in your pocket

CREOLE DELICACIES

MICHELIN
Travel Publications

MAIN CONTRIBUTOR: BEN SANDMEL

PHOTOGRAPH CREDITS
All photographs supplied by The Travel Library:
A Amsel 33, 38; Stuart Black title page, 5, 6, 10, 12, 13,
14, 19, 22, 25, 39, 40, 41, 42, 43, 44, 46, 47, 48, 49, 51, 52,
53, 54, 55, 56, 57, 58, 59, 61, 63, 65, 67, 71, 74, 78, 79, 87,
89, 90, 93, 95, 96, 99, 104, 105, 107(top); Greg Balfour
Evans 28; David Lyons 37, 45, 64, 77, 80, 123; Redferns
97, 98(top, bottom), 101, 109; Redferns/Leon Morris
front cover; Ian Robinson back cover, 9, 27, 29, 30, 31,
50, 66, 69, 70, 73, 75, 82, 84, 102 107(bottom), 113, 115,
116, 121, 125, 126.

*Front cover: Saxophone player by the Mississippi; back cover:
ornate balconies in the French Quarter; title page: Creole
restaurant sign*

MANUFACTURE FRANÇAISE DES PNEUMATIQUES MICHELIN

Place des Carmes-Déchaux – 63000 Clermont-Ferrand (France)

© Michelin et Cie. Propriétaires-Éditeurs 1997

Dépôt légal Mai 97 – ISBN 2-06-651801-8 – ISSN 1272-1689

No part of this publication may be reproduced in any form

without the prior permission of the publisher.

Printed in Spain 09-01/3

MICHELIN TRAVEL PUBLICATIONS
Hannay House
39 Clarendon Road
WATFORD Herts WD17 1JA - UK
☎ (01923) 205240
www.ViaMichelin.com

MICHELIN TRAVEL PUBLICATIONS
Michelin North America
One Parkway South
GREENVILLE, SC 29615
☎ 1-800 423-0485
www.ViaMichelin.com

CONTENTS

INTRODUCTION

New Orleans is one of the most sensual cities in the world – an intriguing, insular world of its own that functions well outside of America's mainstream. Often regarded as the northern frontier of the Caribbean, the 'Crescent City' combines the cultural heritage of West Africa, Cuba and Haiti with the colonial legacies of Spain and France, and the traditions of European immigrants who arrived *en masse* during the 19C. New Orleans' renowned musical and culinary traditions draw on all of these influences, and jazz, rhythm & blues and rich aromas waft in the sultry breeze, along with tropical floral scents and the haunting sound of boat whistles from the Mississippi River.

There is visual intoxication, too, in New Orleans' crazy-quilt assemblage of architectural styles. French, Spanish and West Indian structures prevail in the French Quarter, while classic American styles dominate the Garden District.

Sometimes all these sensory charms converge at neighborhood watering-holes with vintage neon signs, mouth-watering menus and a juke-box full of hometown hits. Eating crawfish-tail and Creole tomato salad, while Fats Domino or Louis Armstrong come blasting out from the corner – this is a great New Orleans moment, an exquisite combination of aesthetic pleasures that can be experienced nowhere else.

Few American cities have such a long and diverse history, with a corresponding variety of historic sites and museums, and no other American city has such a distinctive local culture, blending down-to-earth street activity and old-money elitism.

At its best, New Orleans is cheerfully anarchic. Residents are prone to park their cars on whichever side of the street takes their fancy, regardless of the flow of traffic, and the local dialect takes a similarly whimsical approach to syntax. At Mardi Gras such looseness escalates into mass decadence on a scale that must be seen to be believed.

Yet New Orleans' famed 'Big Easy' ambiance is often accompanied by rampant inefficiency and suspended logic. In addition, the city's numerous social ills and sagging economy have made crime a problem – in all parts of town – so travelers and residents alike must always be vigilant and street-smart. But these problems should not discourage visitors; few destinations compare for a refreshing getaway, a fascinating place for exploration and hedonism. New Orleans can quickly get under your skin, and make anywhere else look very dull indeed.

GEOGRAPHY

New Orleans lies in the south-eastern corner of Louisiana, with the state of Mississippi 30 miles (48km) to the north-east. With a population of 1.5 million, the metropolitan area encompasses six parishes – the Louisiana term for the local government units known as counties in other American states. These are Orleans Parish (the most populous, and home to the city proper), Jefferson, St Bernard, Plaquemines, St Tammany and St Charles. Adjacent to the city, Jefferson Parish was the first to experience the suburban sprawl which has now spread to St Tammany, once a haven for quiet rural living.

A freighter rounds the river bend of the mighty Mississippi.

New Orleans' divergent neighborhoods seem more like an assemblage of small towns. Those sections of most interest to visitors are the French Quarter, the Garden District, Uptown and Mid-City. The **French Quarter**, New Orleans' oldest neighborhood, sits adjacent to the Mississippi River, at the north-eastern upstroke of its curving course through town. The term 'French Quarter' is somewhat of a misnomer, since its renowned 18C architecture is predominantly Spanish. The area has a European flavor rarely found in America, and is home to some of New Orleans' leading museums, hotels, restaurants, nightclubs and shops. Bourbon Street is a notoriously tawdry stretch of bars for all tastes, and 'the Quarter' in general has been marred by a profusion of souvenir and T-shirt shops. But many blocks remain quiet, residential and quite beautiful.

The **Garden District**, located several miles upstream and half a mile in from the river, is equally famous. In contrast to the French Quarter's European flavor, the Garden District is a distinctly American section of ornate, early 19C mansions with vast gardens and a canopy of venerable oak trees. With fewer commercial intrusions and more open space, in many respects, this choice residential enclave is also a prettier section of town.

Further still upriver is a vast section known as **Uptown**, the site of palatial homes from the late 19C and early 20C, Audubon Park, the city's excellent zoo, as well as several of New Orleans' best nightclubs, and shopping that includes specialty stores and numerous antique shops. Across town, midway between the Mississippi and Lake

Pontchartrain, **Mid-City** is full of beautifully restored 19C homes and a huge green space known as City Park where one can row, play golf, ride horses, or visit the New Orleans Museum of Art.

Numerous bodies of water divide metropolitan New Orleans, which is traversed by a network of bridges, causeways, tunnels and ferry boats. There's a popular misconception that New Orleans literally occupies the mouth of the **Mississippi**, where that mighty river empties into the Gulf of Mexico. The city is actually situated north-west of the mouth, some 90 miles (145km) upstream, along a crescent-shaped stretch of river that accounts for one of New Orleans' best-known nicknames, and also creates some logistical chaos.

The Mississippi essentially flows south, and the 'Crescent City' is technically located on its east bank. But the river's eastern-flowing curve at New Orleans makes it the city's *southern* border, while **Lake Pontchartrain** forms the boundary to the north. Because of this peculiar bend, those New Orleans neighborhoods on the river's *west* bank are actually located due *east* of the city's center. Such confusion explains why the four points of the compass are useless for determining directions in New Orleans, and thus are never used. The co-ordinates instead are uptown, downtown, river and lake. By this logic, for example, the Pontchartrain Hotel occupies the downtown-lake corner of St Charles and Jackson Avenues – a precise location that makes immediate sense to locals.

New Orleans is 5ft (1.5m) below sea level, which means the city is extremely prone to flooding. In fact those neighborhoods

Stand on the Moonwalk and marvel as huge ships navigate the killer currents and treacherous bends of the mighty Mississippi. No wonder New Orleans is called 'The Crescent City'.

Sunset on the Mississippi.

nearest to the river and lake are on New Orleans' highest ground, much like the rim of a cup, while the center of town is the lowest. There heavy rain can quickly overwhelm the city's drainage system and fill the streets with several feet of water. Homeowners in New Orleans suffer continual problems with houses that sink and sag, while all coffins are placed in crypts above ground since conventional burial would leave them prone to being unceremoniously washed away.

The Mississippi River is vital to New Orleans' economic survival, ensuring its role as a busy port and enhancing its appeal to tourists. But rivers always seek the shortest route to the sea, and for decades the

Mississippi has been attempting to straighten its meandering course, seeking a new main channel via a smaller but more direct tributary – the **Atchafalaya River** – and thus flowing due south to the Gulf of Mexico. The United States Army Corps of Engineers is spending billions of dollars trying to prevent this re-routing, though it is inevitable over the course of geological time, and could happen instantly in a major flood or an earthquake. If so, New Orleans would sit beside a stagnating back-water, its days as a harbor gone forever.

The low-lying ground around New Orleans is completely flat, and approximately half of its 365 square mile area (587 sq km) is aquatic, with alligators,

The world's longest causeway, crossing Lake Pontchartrain, leads to the rolling hills of the Piney Woods.

egrets and nutria thriving within the city limits. Swampland continues to the east, south and west. The open waters of the Gulf of Mexico are some 45 miles (72km) due east of town – although inaccessible by road – but coastal erosion is continually shrinking this distance as freshwater wetlands give way to the sea. There are no decent beaches near New Orleans within the state of Louisiana, but the Gulf Coast beaches in the state of Mississippi, an hour's drive away, are quite pleasant. North of Lake Pontchartrain, which is traversed by the world's longest causeway at 26 miles (42km), the terrain changes to the gently rolling country known as the **Piney Woods**, with slightly drier air and lower temperatures.

HISTORY

Native Americans (also referred to as Indians) lived in the area for thousands of years before the arrival of the Spanish. Local tribes included the Washa, Cwasha, Tangipahoa, Acolopissa, Chitimacha, Houma and Choctaw. Explorers from Hernando de Soto's Spanish expedition floated past the city's future site in 1543, but did not attempt to establish a settlement. In 1682 the French explorer **La Salle** claimed all land drained by the Mississippi River in the name of France's king, Louis XIV, and named it 'Louisiane' in his honor, but no immediate settlement was attempted. Then, in 1716, a Scottish financier named **John Law** persuaded the French government to invest in developing Louisiane and establishing a local base of operations. Law chose a site with equal access to the Mississippi River and Lake Pontchartrain – which offered a shorter route to the Gulf of

Mexico – and named it after one of his principal patrons, the **Duke of Orleans**. La Nouvelle Orléans was founded in 1718 when its first governor, **Sieur de Bienville**, arrived with a flotilla of six boats carrying craftsmen and convict laborers.

The Foundation of New Orleans

Building a new city in such harsh environs was not easy. Tropical storms blew down the first structures, and the Native Americans responded violently to the seizure of their land. But New Orleans grew as a vital center for trade between Europe, the Caribbean and mainland settlements in the New World. The population swelled steadily, bolstered by an ever-increasing number of slaves brought in bondage from West Africa to grow such profitable crops as cotton and sugar cane.

According to the terms of the Treaty of Paris which ended the Seven Years' War in 1763, France's North American territories were to be turned over to the British. However, the previous year France had

Street signs are poignant reminders of Spanish rule of the city.

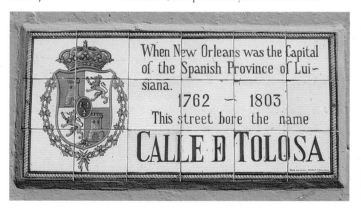

When New Orleans was the Capital of the Spanish Province of Luisiana.

1762 – 1803

This street bore the name

CALLE D TOLOSA

12

The Old Ursuline Convent on Chartres Street was one of the few buildings to survive the great fire of 1788.

secretly ceded the Louisiana Territory to its Spanish ally. Unhappy with this dramatic turn of events, the French community in New Orleans eventually rebelled against **Spanish rule**. Although the Spanish governor was forced to flee, the leaders of the revolt were later executed and Spanish sovereignty re-established. The three-plus decades of Spanish rule that followed brought growth, prosperity and the reconstruction of the city in the aftermath of disastrous fires in 1788 and 1794.

In 1800, another secret agreement returned to French rule the 900 000 square mile (2 331 000 sq km) Louisiana Territory that stretched west of the Mississippi and as far north as the Canadian border. Three years later, French emperor Napoleon

Bonaparte, more interested in establishing his empire in Europe and in need of funds, offered the entire territory to the US government, which concluded the historic **Louisiana Purchase** for a mere $15 million.

American rule was soon challenged by the British in the War of 1812. Although settled by an agreement signed in Europe in December of 1814, word of the peace treaty did not reach Louisiana until after American troops had prevailed at the **Battle of New Orleans** a month later (the battle was actually fought in the present-day suburb of

General Andrew Jackson, hero of the Battle of New Orleans, is honored in Jackson Square by America's first equestrian statue.

Chalmette). The victory made folk heroes of both the American general, **Andrew Jackson**, who went on to become president, and the pirate **Jean Lafitte**, whose outlaw forces rallied behind the American cause.

Tensions

The combination of stable government, the development of shallow-draft steamboats to ply the inland rivers, and New Orleans' continuing growth as a port all led to an ever-increasing influx of English-speaking American settlers. These new residents were shunned by the old-line French and Spanish families but gradually came to dominate New Orleans' business and political affairs. For a time, New Orleans was actually divided into two separate cities, with Canal Street serving as the border between the French and American sections. This gave rise to the term 'neutral ground,' still used today in New Orleans to describe the grassy median area in the middle of a street.

As a major center for the **slave trade**, New Orleans was in the midst of the debate surrounding abolition, and when the **Civil War** erupted in 1861, the city was an important military target. The capture of New Orleans in 1862 by the Federal navy had serious implications for the Confederate cause, and contributed significantly to the South's ultimate defeat. Although the Civil War ended in 1865, Federal troops occupied the city until 1877, and during the post-war era known as **Reconstruction** New Orleans saw more strife and bloodshed than during the actual war.

Racial tension continued through the 19C, as slavery was replaced by stringently enforced **segregation**. A challenge to such laws by a New Orleanian named **Homer Plessy** went all the way to the United States Supreme Court in 1896; the Court ruled in favor of 'separate but equal' facilities for whites and blacks, setting a national precedent that prevailed until the Court reversed its decision in 1954. Nor were black people the only victims of discrimination; resentment towards the city's burgeoning Southern Italian community climaxed in a bloody riot in 1891.

New Orleans in the 20C

By 1900 New Orleans' population was nearly 300 000, and the early 20C saw the city beginning to take on its present form. In the first four decades, high-rises were built in the Business District, recurrent outbreaks of yellow fever were finally conquered by mosquito control, and the port was enhanced by the creation of a canal connecting Lake Pontchartrain with the Mississippi River. **Governor Huey Long**, like many current residents of rural north Louisiana, had little sympathy for the southern part of the state and its principal city. But the road-building and development of oil resources during Long's controversial administration expanded New Orleans' economic base, and made it a center of the petro-chemical industry.

The years after the Second World War found New Orleans grappling with the social turmoil of the Civil Rights era, and trying to hold its own as a center of American commerce. Plans to build a highway through the heart of the historic French Quarter were defeated, as the citizens began to appreciate the city's unique character. At the same time, the opening of the Louisiana Superdome in 1970 transformed the face of the Central Business District, and gave the city a world-class venue for major sporting events and conventions. During the 1980s the oil business skyrocketed and then plummeted, throwing the regional economy into a serious depression. City authorities wisely chose to concentrate on the steady appeal of tourism and conventions as primary economic assets, and an impressive new convention center was built. A far less profitable decision was made in 1991 when the state legislature legalized gambling, and approved construction of the world's largest casino in the heart of New Orleans. The developer declared bankruptcy before the casino's completion, and the building remained unfinished for more than a year at the foot of Canal Street. A refinancing plan was approved in 1998, and the casino finally opened in 1999, although today financial instability renders its future uncertain.

New Orleans remains beset by crime, a poorly-educated workforce and a sluggish economy. But newly-elected officials seem sincerely dedicated to bringing the Crescent City into the 21C with pragmatic reverence for both its rich past and future potential.

THE PEOPLE AND CULTURE

Although the New Orleans area was inhabited by **Native Americans** at the time of European settlement, there is no visible Indian community in the city today. But the Indians' cultural legacy is evident in such names as Tchoupitoulas Street, and culinary customs, including the ground sassafras seasoning known as *filé* powder. In addition, there is a fascinating convergence of Native American and African-American cultures in the Mardi Gras 'Indian' tradition (*see* p.31).

Americans are fond of describing their nation as a 'melting pot' consisting of myriad nationalities, religions, and ethnic and racial groups, with the common bond of US citizenship. There is no better example of this concept than New Orleans, despite a popular misconception that it is solely a city of French ancestry. France was the first source of **European settlers**, of course, and contributed multiple waves of immigration from various regions over the years. But the early French colonists were soon joined by Spanish colonists and followed, over the next two centuries, by significant numbers of immigrants from the four corners of the globe.

Huge numbers of unwilling immigrants from West Africa were brought to New Orleans as slaves, and though many were dispersed around the South after being sold, New Orleans retains an **African-American** population of approximately 62 per cent. Many blacks and whites alike arrived from the island now known as Haiti during the 1790s, following a slave rebellion; some of these black immigrants were slaves, while others were slave-owners. Folklorists regard New Orleans and South Louisiana as America's richest region of African cultural retention. This is not only because New Orleans had a large slave population, but also because the city's slave-owners were far more tolerant than their Anglo counterparts in other regions of the South. Instead of suppressing every trace of African culture in order to force the slaves into greater compliance, the masters of New Orleans allowed their chattels to gather on Sundays to socialize, dance and make music. Much of the music played at these gatherings – which

were held just outside of the French Quarter, at a place called Congo Square – was centered around African drumming, although many New World influences and instruments also crept in over time. The African aesthetics that were nurtured there contributed to the development of both jazz and rhythm & blues, and are still reflected in the city's musical evolution. African culinary traditions are also a major component in New Orleans cuisine, along with the native cookery of France, Italy and the West Indies.

Music transcends age and ethnic differences in the melting pot of New Orleans.

The term **Creole** is often heard in discussions of the people and culture of New Orleans, and is just as often used incorrectly. Creole originally referred to people of French or Spanish ancestry who were born in New Orleans; this usage specified white people, and wealthy ones from old-line families at that. In the 19C, Creole also came to refer to light-skinned black people who spoke French, and who regarded themselves as quite distinct from both whites and darker-skinned blacks. Today, the term Creole is used in both senses, and in a broader sense it can be applied to anyone born in Louisiana. Yet Creole is a word that continues to spark sharp controversy both in New Orleans proper and throughout southern Louisiana, revealing a complex web of racial and socio-economic prejudices. Those who consider themselves Creole, by whatever definition, often bristle when it is claimed by others. To further complicate matters, Creole has evolved in recent years to denote the French-speaking black people of rural south-western Louisiana, some 100 miles (161km) west of New Orleans. These people are the black counterparts of their white neighbors, the Cajuns (*see* opposite).

The **Islenos**, as the descendants of Canary Island immigrants are known, constitute one of New Orleans' most unique communities. This relatively small community left its home off the coast of West Africa around 1780, and settled in the salt marshes of St Bernard Parish. Although only 30 miles (48km) from New Orleans, this rural area has remained isolated, with fishing and fur-trapping the main occupations. Incredibly enough, the residents' 18C Spanish dialect has survived to this day – although they all speak English, as well – as have many of their epic medieval folksongs, known as *decimas.*

New Orleans is also home to a sizable, long-standing Jewish community, and large communities of recent immigrants from Cuba. Various other ethnic and cultural groups are established in the city as well, and contribute to New Orleans' diverse population – the Italians, with their exquisite Mediterranean cuisine, and colorful feast days; the Vietnamese, whose extensive gardens in New Orleans East make the neighborhood resemble an Asian village; the Yugoslav oystermen of Plaquemines Parish; and the recent immigrants from El Salvador, who have opened restaurants known as *pupuserias* on the West Bank.

Cajun derives from the term **Acadian**. The Acadians were French-speaking residents of Acadia (in present-day Nova Scotia), expelled by the British after they refused to pledge their allegiance to the British Crown. Dispersed from their homeland, large numbers of Acadians eventually came to Louisiana, but they did not settle down within the urban French community in New Orleans. Instead, the Acadians took to the rural swamps and prairies to the west, where their culture remained remarkably self-contained until the oil boom of the 1930s brought the outside world rushing in.

As a result of this long isolation the Cajuns' 18C French dialect was preserved, and is still spoken today by several hundred thousand people, both white and black; almost all of them know English as well, but for many it is a second language. French was so dominant during the last century, in fact, that immigrants to the region who had English names such as Johnson would frequently change to a Gallicized spelling, such as Jeansonne. The black Creole dialect of the region has many Afro-Caribbean features that distinguish it from Cajun French, and the Cajun and Creole spoken today in south-western Louisiana are both quite different from the French which once flourished in New Orleans. This underscores the fact that the Cajuns are not native to New Orleans and represent a distinct cultural community, even though popular films such as *The Big Easy* tend to lump the two regions together.

Against the rich backdrop of New Orleans' turbulent history, the city's diverse and passionate people are clearly its greatest

Music on Royal Street.

resource. Thrown together in this isolated corner of the New World, these diverse people absorbed each others' languages, customs, culinary and musical traditions, and much more. What eventually evolved, in classic melting pot fashion, was the distinctive regional culture of New Orleans. This culture continues to thrive today – eccentric, iconoclastic, and proud of it – despite New Orleans' complete access to cable television, the information superhighway, and every other potentially homogenizing influence. While New Orleans certainly has its share of prejudice and racial and ethnic conflict, the city is equally notable for its cultural commonality and the frequency of contact between people of differing backgrounds. Far less rigidly segregated than northern cities such as Chicago and Boston, New Orleans' blacks and whites often live close together, sharing many customs, speech patterns, musical and food preferences, and the like.

Another unique product of New Orleans' diversity is the city's accent. It is quite different from a stereotypical Southern drawl – in fact New Orleanians are often mistaken for New Yorkers. New Orleans-speak combines Northern pronunciation with Southern/African-American grammar. This regional anomaly is thought to be a legacy of the city's Irish immigrants, most of whom first came to America via such northern ports of entry as New York and Boston. And speaking of accents and pronunciations, locals never refer to their city as 'New Or-LEENS', but rather as 'New OR-lins', 'New OR-lee-uns' or 'Nuh-wawlins.' Curiously, however, Orleans Avenue and Orleans Parish are pronounced 'Or-LEENS.'

Voodoo

Voodoo is one of the most exotic stereotypical images associated with New Orleans, and one that is also prone to exaggeration and exploitation. In fact, voodoo is a religion combining elements of Catholicism with the spiritual beliefs of such West African tribes as the Fon and the Yoruba. These beliefs were a great source of strength to African slaves in the New World; they were expressed through intense rituals, including drumming and animal sacrifice, which offered emotional release from the harsh circumstances of bondage. When voodoo also became a rallying force in slave uprisings in Haiti in the late 18C and early 19C, the governor of Louisiana banned the importation of slaves who practised it – but the tradition was already firmly established.

During the 19C, mother and daughter 'voodoo queens' both named **Marie Laveau** enjoyed considerable social and political power on all levels of New Orleans society; what are thought to be their graves in St Louis Cemetery No 1 are still frequently visited. Another prominent voodoo figure from this era was **Dr John Creaux**, a name which was adopted in the 1960s by the popular New Orleans rhythm & blues pianist, Mac Rebennack.

In present-day New Orleans there are still a significant number of people who believe in and practise some form of voodoo, but exactly how many is difficult to say since it is a highly secretive sub-culture. Although spells are not being cast on every street corner, as depicted in popular films such as *Angel Heart*, there are occasional reports of people being arrested in cemeteries with knives and live chickens.

Stores dealing in charms and potions, such as the **F & F Botanica** (801 N Broad Street) attract a steady clientele; many customers are recent arrivals from the Caribbean who practise a related religion known as *santeria*. The spiritualist churches within New Orleans' black community combine African and voodoo-related beliefs with Christianity. There is a **Voodoo Museum** in the French Quarter (*see* p.64).

Voodoo masks and charms on display in the Voodoo Museum.

MARDI GRAS

Mardi Gras is a time when all of New Orleans' extremes and superlatives converge in one massive season of celebration. Literally meaning 'Fat Tuesday', Mardi Gras is the day before Ash Wednesday – the beginning of Lent, when worldly pleasures are renounced for spiritual introspection. Accordingly, Fat Tuesday represents a final period of sensual indulgence before this abstinence begins. In hedonistic New Orleans, pre-Lenten celebrations begin almost immediately after the Christmas holidays, so that Mardi Gras is actually a multi-week celebration – known as Carnival in many countries – rather than just a single-day event.

During this time, New Orleans' high frivolity boils over into complete pandemonium. Several seasonal anthems – Professor Longhair's *Mardi Gras In New Orleans*, Al Johnson's *Carnival Time*, and *Second Line* by Stop, Inc. – are played repeatedly on the radio and over loudspeakers, creating a virtually continuous sonic blur. There are over 40 massive parades that tie up the city's principal thoroughfares, and anyone attempting to conduct serious business must plan their day around avoiding closed-off streets. The tens of thousands who do attend the parades often stake out their vantage points hours in advance, if not the night before, camping out on the neutral ground and celebrating 'Carnival' with beer, boiled crawfish and the seasonal confection known as 'king cake'.

The parades, which last for hours, consist of elaborate, multi-tiered floats occupied by costumed riders who thrill the crowds by tossing plastic necklaces and trinkets known

as 'throws.' Adults who are otherwise quite sensible will risk life and limb to catch this ersatz jewelry and bedeck themselves with it, dozens of times over. Many such spectators don elaborate costumes, ranging from traditional clown suits to kinky erotic outfits. In a related vein, it is common for heterosexual males to beseech women to bare their breasts, while many gay men delight in extremely skimpy costumes which

At Mardi Gras, the streets of New Orleans become an exuberant display of colorful costumes and music.

manage to be quite elaborate, despite their brevity. New Orleans' gay community is most visible in the upper French Quarter and the adjoining Faubourg Marigny.

Face painting is offered on street corners.

Each Mardi Gras parade is organized by a club known as a krewe – a deliberate misspelling of 'crew' – which emerged in the 19C. With such fanciful names as The Krewe of Poseidon and The Krewe of Bacchus, these organizations poke fun at pomp and circumstance while simultaneously revelling in it. Some people derive a sense of self-

The Mardi Gras floats are sure to provide a colorful display.

importance from joining a krewe, and some krewes are quite exclusive, if not downright elitist. Until recently, some krewes were also segregated, barring membership on racial and religious grounds, until a city ordinance banned parades by krewes that discriminated. In tradition-bound New Orleans, this was a very controversial issue. Several krewes opened their ranks, but three prominent ones cancelled their parades. One, the Krewe of Proteus, has since resumed parading but the Krewes of Momus and Comus continue to celebrate Mardi Gras with private balls.

Parades are banned from the French Quarter, because of the risks associated with over-crowding in the narrow streets. Canal Street is one of the best vantage points for the main parades, but they can also be seen along St Charles Avenue between Napoleon Avenue and Canal Street; Napoleon Avenue between Freret and Tchoupitoulas; and Carrollton Avenue between Orleans Avenue and Canal Street. For a comparatively uncrowded scene, the Thoth parade, near

Audubon Park, is recommended.

Mardi Gras parades also feature marching bands, military revues, clowns, equestrian teams and *flambeaux* – flaming torches carried by marchers that give the spectacle a haunting quality. In addition to such flamboyant street action, Mardi Gras is an important social season of glamorous balls, which may cost wealthy participants tens of thousands of dollars. Not surprisingly, Mardi Gras has become a major contributor to the local economy; hotels and restaurants are booked to capacity for several weeks, while bead stores and float builders stay busy all year. Numerous books exist on the subject,

The colors, the goodwill, the begging for beads from a passing parade – you can't understand Mardi Gras without experiencing the New Orleans version.

the Presbytère houses a permanent Mardi Gras musuem (*see* p.41), and local television stations retain resident Mardi Gras experts for nightly commentary during the height of the season.

One of the most fascinating traditions takes place within the black community, as the Mardi Gras 'Indians' parade and chant, bedecked in their elaborate hand-sewn costumes, replete with sequins, ornate beadwork and pastel plumes. These 'Indians' are not Native Americans, but their costumes incorporate Native American motifs, the 'tribes' have Indian names such as the Yellow Pocahontas, and the leader of each tribe is known as 'the Big Chief'. In a sense, the tribes function as a combination men's club/fraternal organization, and a sense of community pride is fostered when the tribe parades through the neighborhood, stopping at each corner tavern for a toast and a chant. The Indian chants, drum beats and costumes have parallels in the Carnival traditions of the Caribbean.

MUST SEE

There is much to see and do in New Orleans, depending on the time of year you visit and your personal interests. Below we suggest a few essential attractions and experiences for the first-time visitor.

The French Quarter★★★

The French Quarter is a delightful place to explore at will, starting from the heart of the district, Jackson Square, but a guided walking tour with one of the qualified companies is the best way to learn about this neighborhood's rich history, legends and architecture. The buggy drivers who give tours of 'the Quarter' are notoriously inaccurate, but a carriage ride at twilight can still be quite entertaining and/or romantic.

Audubon Zoo and the Zoo Cruise★★

The Audubon Zoo is one of America's best, with such features as the Louisiana Swamp Exhibit and the African Savannah. A return voyage downtown on the Mississippi River, from the zoo in Audubon Park to the French Quarter, through New Orleans' busy harbor, is the perfect complement to a streetcar ride uptown.

Jean Lafitte National Historical Park/Swamp Tour

Stroll along the boardwalk trails, through the primordial swamp at the Barataria Unit of Jean Lafitte National Historical Park (6588 Barataria Blvd, Marrero, La). Surrounded by egrets, alligators and dense sub-tropical foliage you can easily imagine the intimidating environment that confronted New Orleans' first settlers. Or, try one of the many excellent swamp tours on offer.

Plantation Visit★★

Take a day trip along the Great River Road
to one of the beautifully restored mansion
homes, such as Oak Alley, complete with

*Street musicians on
Royal Street, in the
heart of the French
Quarter.*

antiques, sumptuous furnishings, and often
with a costumed guide.

The Garden District★★★
Always fashionable, this stunningly beautiful
neighborhood has become especially trendy
of late, thanks to such celebrity residents as
novelist Anne Rice and rock star Trent
Reznor. Predominately residential, the
Garden District has fewer contemporary
distractions from the charms of a bygone
era.

The Louisiana State Museum★★
Housed in three historic French Quarter
buildings – the Presbytère, the Cabildo and
the Old US Mint – this complex features a
varied rotation of exhibits, and extensive
permanent displays on New Orleans'
political and social history, and such cultural
phenomena as jazz and Mardi Gras.

St Charles Avenue Streetcar★★
Perhaps the loveliest stretch of public
transportation in America, the 6.5 mile
(10.4km) trip from Canal and St Charles to
Carrollton and Claiborne is an
indispensable part of any visit to New
Orleans – both for the beautiful Garden
District homes and scenery *en route*, and the
experience of sitting in impeccably restored
trolley cars.

Café du Monde
An ideal spot for writing postcards home,
people-watching, or just taking in the sights
of Jackson Square, Café du Monde, in the
heart of the French Quarter, is perpetually
open for strong 'New Orleans blend' coffee
with chicory, and beignets, a fried-dough

pastry dusted with powder sugar. The combined jolt of sweets and caffeine will fortify you for hours of sightseeing.

Voodoo Sites and St Louis Cemeteries★

Known as 'cities of the dead,' New Orleans' vast 18C cemeteries – with their above-ground burial vaults and French inscriptions – are one of the city's most intriguing features. But they are located in dangerous neighborhoods, and should not be visited alone. The same is true of some of the prime sites associated with voodoo. You should explore these facets of the city with a guided tour.

City Park and the Victorian Carousel★

Children and the young at heart will be delighted by a spin astride the fanciful creatures of this vintage merry-go-round, which has been painstakingly restored to its original 1906 condition. The vast grounds of City Park offer many other attractions as well.

A Jazz Performance

The musical genre which experienced some of its most important developments in New Orleans continues to flourish and evolve today, and you should try to see at least one performance at Preservation Hall, the Palm Court Jazz Café or Donna's Bar & Grill, or attend the Jazz and Heritage Festival if it coincides with your visit. These three French Quarter nightspots are not the only places to hear New Orleans jazz, but they concentrate on it exclusively, with performances every night of the week, featuring the best of the city's established musicians and up-and-coming young players.

THE FRENCH QUARTER★★★

The best way to get a feel for the French Quarter is to take a leisurely daytime stroll around the area. Leave firm plans and hard facts for the guided tours that are also recommended (*see* p.68) and let New Orleans' sensory barrage direct your route. 'The Quarter', or 'Vieux Carré', is best explored on foot, and there is far too much traffic to do so effectively by car. Despite its name, the district has a Spanish feel to it, since fires in 1788 and 1794 destroyed almost all of the French settlement.

It is a lively, bustling place, at times verging on the rowdy. The area is bordered by Canal Street, Esplanade Avenue, Rampart Street and the Mississippi River. **Bourbon Street★**, the best known thoroughfare, is a tawdry assemblage of strip clubs, bars and souvenir shops; even so, some excellent musicians perform there nightly, and it is also the location of some fine restaurants. **Royal Street★★** is world-renowned for its connoisseur-class antique shops, but antiques at a fraction of Royal Street prices are found along the lower end of Decatur Street, near Esplanade. The cross streets in this section of the French Quarter – Barracks, Governor Nicholls, Ursulines – are mainly residential.

Again, a word of caution about crime is unfortunately necessary. Keep aware of people around you, and do not venture into isolated areas, or into the neighborhood across Rampart Street heading away from the river. Two of New Orleans' most famous cemeteries are in this area (St Louis No 1 and No 2) but they should not be visited without a guided tour.

Jackson Square Area★

With an area of some 96 city blocks, the Quarter has many different facets to explore, and **Café du Monde** (800 Decatur Street) is an excellent place to start, savoring the essence of the place over coffee and beignets. From this central point, the Quarter's most worthwhile sites are all just minutes away.

Across Decatur Street from the Café is **Jackson Square★★**, long regarded as the very heart of the city. The square was named after Andrew Jackson, the hero of the Battle of New Orleans, 1815, and the massive statue of Jackson on horseback forms the centrepiece of the square. Mimes, portrait artists and street-musicians all ply their trades in Jackson Square, and many are very

The legendary Café du Monde has been the place to take coffee and beignets for decades.

The stately St Louis Cathedral soars above Jackson Square.

talented. Jackson Square has also inspired such major talents as Tennessee Williams and William Faulkner, who lived just behind it in 1925; Faulkner's former apartment at 624 Pirates Alley now houses the **Faulkner House** bookstore and a literary society in his honor.

William Faulkner, one of New Orleans' famous literary personalities, lived in this house along Pirates Alley.

Jackson Square is surrounded by some of the city's most impressive buildings. The imposing **St Louis Cathedral★**, built in 1851, is America's oldest active Roman Catholic church. The original wooden church, built on the site in 1727, was destroyed by fire in 1788. Inside, the six stained-glass windows depicting the Life of St Louis were a gift from Spain. Look also for the spectacular painting of St Louis declaring the Seventh Crusade, which spans the walls and ceiling behind the altar. The cathedral is open daily, and tours are available.

The **Cabildo★★** and the **Presbytère★★** are classic Spanish colonial structures dating from 1795 that flank the cathedral and which now form part of the **Louisiana State Museum★★** (*see* p.63). The Cabildo, with its mansard roof and dormer windows, has in the past served a variety of functions, including French police station and guardhouse, statehouse of the Spanish

The interior of St Louis Cathedral, with its fine ceiling frescoes.

government, City Hall and Louisiana's State Supreme Court. Its stately rooms now provide a fitting setting for its historical exhibits. The Presbytère, similar in design to the Cabildo, was originally built to house priests from the cathedral (though it was never used for this). It now houses a fascinating and extensive Mardi Gras museum.

The **Pontalba Apartments**★ are two sets of three-storey row houses built in 1849 and 1851 on opposite sides of the square, and represent some of the oldest apartment buildings in the US. The houses were originally financed by the colorful figure Baroness Micaela Almonester de Pontalba, and her initials 'A' and 'P' can be seen in the

The Pontalba Apartments, with their street-level arcaded shops.

The walk along the river to Woldenberg Park offers panoramic views across the river.

ornate ironwork which adorns the façades. There are arcaded shops below, with apartments above (now much sought after); one houses a branch of the **Louisiana Office of Tourism** (☎ 568-5661). The **1850 House**★ has been restored and furnished authentically, and provides a fascinating insight into the daily life of 19C upper-class Creoles.

Behind Café du Monde and on top of the flood-protection embankment of the levee, the brick walkway known as the **Moonwalk** offers a panoramic view of the Mississippi River and its dramatic curve around Algiers Point on the opposite shore. Relax on a park bench and watch the frenetic activity of New Orleans' harbor, or walk upriver (towards the bridges) into **Woldenberg Park**. This 16 acre (6.5ha) area of grass, trees, shrubs and statuary offers a tranquil retreat in the heart of New Orleans.

The promenade along the river leads on to the **Aquarium of the Americas★★**, with its slanted, blue-green oculus, and the adjacent IMAX theatre (*see* p.65).

The Aquarium of the Americas, with the modern city skyline beyond.

EXPLORING NEW ORLEANS

One block past this aquatic paradise is the **Canal Street ferry landing**; the short round-trip across the river, free to pedestrians, is one of New Orleans' most delightful and scenic bargains. One block inland, there is excellent contemporary shopping along North Peters Street, while a further two blocks in, on Royal Street between Iberville and St Louis Street, a stretch of fine antique shops cater for well-heeled collectors. Heading back towards the river on St Louis Street, the **Napoleon House★** (about 1815), with its classic New Orleans combination of faded grandeur and time-warp ambiance, beckons you to step in for a drink.

Royal Street is noted for its elegant buildings, many with fine wrought-iron balconies.

Rainy day? Try a Pimm's cup at Napoleon House, while opera music plays in the background.

Just around the corner you'll find the **Jean Lafitte National Historical Park and Preserve Visitor Center** (419 Decatur Street). The center features excellent exhibits on the unique natural and cultural heritage of Louisiana's Mississippi Delta region, as well as information on the park's other units in the swamps of Barataria (*see* pp.70, 72), at the Chalmette Battlefield (*see* p.74) and in the Cajun Country. Ranger-led tours of the French Quarter depart from here daily (*see* p.68).

French Colonial Area

The few buildings that remain from New Orleans' original French colonial era are all on the downstream side of Café du Monde (heading away from the Mississippi River bridges) in the Quarter's predominantly residential section. One of the earliest buildings in the city is the bar known as **Lafitte's Blacksmith Shop★**, at 941 Bourbon Street; the blacksmith's shop was, according to legend, a front for Jean and Pierre

Lafitte's notorious smuggling and slave-trading activities. **Madame John's Legacy** (632 Dumaine) is sometimes claimed as the oldest building on the Mississippi River, and represents a splendid example of a French 'raised-cottage' structure. It is part of the Louisiana State Museum and is regularly open to the public.

The **Millenberger houses** in the 900 block of Royal Street are prime examples of New Orleans' ornate wrought-iron balconies, a legacy of the Spanish period, while 915 Royal is notable for the cornstalk motif of its wrought-iron fence. A pattern of oak boughs

Fresh Louisiana produce being unloaded at the French Market.

and acorns adorns the ironwork at the **LaBranche House** (700 Royal Street). Take them all in – along with the Quarter's other sights, sounds and aromas – as you amble through the neighborhood, then head towards the river via the funky-but-chic shops of lower Decatur Street, and on to the **French Market**.

The flea market is crammed full of colorful and varied stalls.

The French Market★

This historic complex dates back to the city's earliest days of commerce. It is best known for its continually open produce stands, specializing in such regional delicacies as Opelousas yams, sugar cane, and Creole tomatoes. Sunrise is an especially interesting time of day, when the market is buzzing with purchasers from New Orleans' leading restaurants, and street-vendors loading their battered pick-up trucks. The French Market is also home to a fine **flea market**, with a wide variety of merchandise; some stalls are open daily, while Saturdays and Sundays see a profusion of weekend merchants.

At the upriver tip of the French Market is **Latrobe Park**, a small oasis where jazz bands often perform. Continuing upriver, between the French Market and Café du Monde, the temporary visitor center of the **New Orleans Jazz National Historical Park** (916 N Peters St) hosts live jazz performances on weekends. The park will move to its permanent home in Armstrong Park in 2003.

BEYOND THE FRENCH QUARTER

This route makes a great circle through New Orleans and brings you back to the French Quarter's downriver border, on Esplanade Avenue.

The Spanish Plaza was a Bicentennial gift to the city from Spain in 1976.

Central Business District

Leaving the French Quarter and crossing Canal Street brings you into the Central Business District, usually referred to as the

The World Trade Center provides this spectacular view of the city.

CBD. This is New Orleans' commercial and administrative nerve-center. Most of the major chain hotels are located in this section, as is the city's ultra-modern **Ernest N Morial Convention Center** (Convention Center Boulevard). The second largest convention center in the US, the facilities are in great demand and the center is continually booked. Near the center lies **Spanish Plaza**, one of four foreign squares paying tribute to the role the Spanish, French, British and Italian nations played in the city's history.

Moving away from the river along Poydras Street, you cannot miss the imposing sight of

the **Louisiana Superdome★**. The largest indoor sports arena in the world, the dome is 680ft (210m) across, and the arena can seat 76 000. As well as sporting events, trade shows, theatrical productions and concerts are all held here. Guided tours daily (☎ 587 3808).

The futuristic Louisiana Superdome resembles a giant spaceship at night.

The Warehouse District★

Upriver from the CBD lies the Warehouse District, a recently renovated post-industrial area that was gentrified during the 1984 World's Fair. It is now home to fine restaurants, condominiums, and many of New Orleans' nationally recognized art galleries. The district is very popular with artists, especially between Julia Street (the heart of the district) and St Joseph Street. The modern complex at the **Contemporary Arts Center** (900 Camp Street) houses art

The Contemporary Arts Center building is just as impressive as the exhibits it houses.

The city of New Orleans ran out of money before the construction of the Gallier Hall had reached basement level; it was several years before sufficient funds were raised to complete the magnificent building we see today.

exhibitions and a variety of performances. Further along Camp Street (No 929) is the **Confederate Museum★**, paying steadfast homage to the past (*see* p.66). Across the street is the massive new **National D-Day Museum** (945 Magazine Street; *see* p.66).

Fronting Lee Circle, the **Ogden Museum of Southern Art** (615 Howard Av), housing an important collection of works by Southern artists from the 18C-20C, will open its doors in late 2001. Another highlight of this area is the Greek Revival splendor of the **Gallier Hall** (545 St Charles Ave). Built between

1845 and 1853 by James Gallier Sr, it was New Orleans' City Hall for over 100 years.

The Garden District★★★

Continuing upriver, and crossing under the twin bridges known collectively as the Crescent City Connection, the next major area of interest is **Magazine Street★★**. This contains some of the city's more innovative galleries, jewelry shops and antique stores. The early 19C structures along the 1800-2000 blocks of Magazine Street is known as **Magazine Row**.

Magazine Street leads into the **Garden**

A house on Magazine Street undergoing restoration.

District, bounded on its other three sides by Jackson, Louisiana and St Charles Avenues. The verdant opulence of this 19C district attests to the great success enjoyed by the English-speaking settlers disdainfully referred to as 'les Américains,' when New Orleans was at its peak as a center of commerce and culture. None of the Garden District mansions are open for tours, but simply viewing their ornate exteriors is an aesthetic delight. This is best done on foot, although traffic conditions also make it manageable by car. A drive along Prytania Street, the main thoroughfare, will give you a good feel for the area, with its splendid houses and buildings.

This beautifully maintained Greek Revival house on St Charles Avenue is typical of the architectural splendor of the Garden District.

Aboveground tombs in Lafayette Cemetery.

The predominant style is Greek Revival, with an abundance of grand columns and fanlights, but you will also see architectural delights in Italianate and Queen Anne styles. The many impressive houses include **Colonel Short's Villa** at 1448 Fourth Street, with its 'cornstalk' wrought-iron fence; the Gothic Revival **Briggs-Staub House**, at 2605 Prytania; the Greek Revival **Adams House**, with its curved gallery, at 2423 Prytania; and the **Toby-Westfeldt House**, a raised cottage from the 1830s, at 2340 Prytania. At the residence of **Anne Rice** (1239 First Street), the author of the popular vampire stories, black-clad enthusiasts often congregate in hope of glimpsing their idol.

While in the Garden District, you may care to stop off at the delectable restaurant **Commander's Palace** (1403 Washington Ave), favorite of the locals. Opposite is the historic **Lafayette Cemetery**, with some extraordinarily elaborate aboveground tombs, so typical of New Orleans. However,

Narrow-fronted shotgun houses were designed to minimise the tax payable.

for safety reasons it is not advisable to wander round the cemetery alone.

Between the Garden District and the Mississippi River is a working-class section known as the **Irish Channel**, because it was populated by Irish in the 19C. Here, another classic type of 19C New Orleans architecture prevails. 'Shotgun houses' are so named because they are only one room wide, and all their doors are aligned so that a bullet could be fired in the front door and come cleanly out the back, provided the occupant stood to one side. A fraction of the size of most Garden District mansions, shotgun houses tend to be quite narrow, because New Orleans' property taxes used to be based on street frontage, rather than total area.

Uptown

On the upriver side of Louisiana Avenue, the Garden District proper gives way to **Uptown**. This vast section is quite varied, with sections that in turn are old, new, affluent and impoverished; if you're on foot, keep in mind that such conditions change rapidly. The best way to travel to the Garden District and Uptown is via the **St Charles Avenue streetcar★★**, which will take you past many notable landmarks along the Avenue.

Take a ride on a St Charles Avenue streetcar and explore the sights of the Garden District in style.

The aptly named **Columns Hotel** (3811 St Charles Avenue) was built in 1884 and prominently featured in the film *Pretty Baby*. Equally distinct are the Gothic gables of the **Rayne Memorial Methodist Church**, built in 1875. The vast **Sacred Heart Academy**, with its huge columns and wrap-around porches, is a prestigious girls' school. The Romanesque Revival **Brown Mansion** was one of the most expensive homes to be built in this neighborhood.

Loyola University, the largest Catholic university in the South, was founded in 1840. It occupies a number of buildings forming a square facing onto St Charles Avenue. The neighboring **Tulane University**

The imposing buildings of Loyola University.

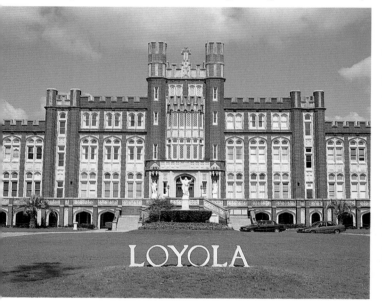

is slightly older, dating from 1834. Housed in impressive Victorian buildings, it is highly regarded for its schools of medicine and law.

Opposite the universities is one of the city's greatest open areas, **Audubon Park★★**. The park is named after John James Audubon, the famous naturalist painter who spent many years in New Orleans. Designed by Frederick Law Olmsted (who also landscaped New York's Central Park), the park contains some wonderful live oak trees, whose spreading boughs form shaded walkways.

Audubon Zoo★★ is quite rightly regarded as one of America's best, with more than 1 500 animals. Wander along wooden walkways through the Louisiana Swamp Exhibit, and spot the rare white alligators;

The live oak trees in Audubon Park provide welcome shade from the summer sun.

take the miniature train through the African Savannah, and view the hippos and rhinos; in the Australian Outback you can see kangaroos, wallabies and emus.

In addition to its excellent zoo, Audubon Park has a golf course, tennis courts, baseball diamonds, stables, and a great view of the river for those who never tire of simply watching the flow. This stretch of the park behind the zoo also includes the boat landing for the **Zoo Cruise**. Departing from Audubon Park and the Riverwalk, in front of the Aquarium, the sternwheeler *John James Audubon* takes you along the Mississippi, and round the port, making stops at the Zoo and the Aquarium. You can buy tickets for one or both attractions, and can choose one-way or return trips; the ride is recommended, whether or not you visit the zoo.

Continuing uptown, past Audubon Park and the limestone façade of Tulane University, beautiful homes line St Charles Avenue until the street ends at the Mississippi River, in a section known as the **Riverbend**, which features some of the city's best shopping. The streetcar route makes a great turn to the right on Carrollton Avenue and continues on for another mile or so, although the surroundings grow increasingly more mundane. If you continue along Carrollton for several miles, however, crossing under Interstate 10, you will re-emerge into worthwhile territory for exploration, namely **Mid-City** and **Faubourg St John**.

Mid-City

This section is less spectacularly opulent than the Garden District and Uptown, but is quite charming all the same. It is a long walk from the French Quarter or Central Business District, so go by car, cab or on the Esplanade or Canal Street bus lines. The fine old homes on **Esplanade Avenue** were once the heart of the city's French community, in the days when they took pains to distinguish themselves from 'les Américains' in the Garden District. The French painter **Edgar Degas** lived at No 2306 between 1872 and 1873, and finished 17 paintings there. Today, the **Degas House**, built in 1852, is a bed-and-breakfast.

At the northern end of Esplanade Avenue

The Victorian Carousel in City Park provides an exciting and nostalgic trip.

is the vast **City Park★**, some 1 500 acres (607ha) of lush, naturally landscaped greenery and lagoons, making it the fifth largest urban park in the US. Created from an area which was once the Louis Allard plantation, the park contains huge old live oaks (some over 800 years old), draped with trailing Spanish moss. Interspersed with lagoons, ponds and streams, it really is a beautiful spot.

The park has many attractions to offer, too. There is the **New Orleans Museum of Art★** (*see* p.66), the 10 acre (4ha) **Botanical Gardens**, boating and fishing, four golf courses, a miniature railway, tennis courts, baseball diamonds, soccer, riding stables and children's rides. The magnificent Victorian **Carousel**, centrepiece of the **Carousel Gardens** amusement park, offers an exciting nostalgic ride. **Storyland**, a 3-D re-creation of popular children's tales, is also a great favorite with young visitors. Whether you are looking for peace and tranquillity, exercise, culture or entertainment, City Park is sure to have something to suit.

A beautiful footpath winds along **Bayou St John**, through the neighborhood on the downtown-river side of the park. On the banks of the bayou sits the **Pitot House Museum** (1440 Moss Street), a West Indies plantation-style home. Built in the 1770s and restored with period furnishings, it is open for tours on a limited schedule (☎ 482-0312 for the schedule). A mile or so away is the headquarters of the **Zulu Social Aid and Pleasure Club** (732 N Broad), an important institution within New Orleans' black community, because of its active participation in Mardi Gras and year-round community action.

MUSEUMS

FRENCH QUARTER
Louisiana State Museum★★
(Various locations; ☎ 568-6968)
The museum is divided into three sections, housed in separate buildings. The **Cabildo**★★ houses permanent displays of Louisiana's history, from colonial days through to the Reconstruction. Fire damaged the building in 1988, but most of the exhibits were saved, including Napoleon's death mask, Mississippi steamboat artifacts and early settler exhibits. The **Presbytère**★★ houses an extensive museum on the history, culture and traditions of Mardi Gras in New Orleans and the surrounding regions. Historic artifacts, plus video interviews and footage from 'Fat Tuesday' celebrations give visitors a taste of the raucous events of the Carnival season. The **Old US Mint** building, on Esplanade Avenue, houses permanent exhibits on jazz and temporaty exhibits of pieces from the state museum's varied collection, and is also used for frequent lectures and musical performances.

Hermann-Grima House
(820 St Louis Street; open Mon-Fri 10am-3.30pm; ☎ 525-5661)
This painstakingly restored American-style townhouse (1831)

The history of slavery exhibit, in the Cabildo Museum.

Staff in period costumes guide you through the Pharmacy Museum.

offers a detailed look at life in New Orleans in the 1830s, including a fully functioning kitchen; Creole cooking demonstrations are held on Thursdays (winter only).

Musée Conti Wax Museum★

(917 Conti Street; open daily 10am-5.30pm, except Thanksgiving Day, Christmas week and the week of Mardi Gras; ☎ 525-2605)
In the grand tradition of Madame Tussaud's, over 100 of Louisiana's historical figures are immortalized here, including Andrew Jackson, Jean Lafitte and Marie Laveau.

Voodoo Museum

(724 Dumaine Street; open daily 10am-8pm; ☎ 523-7685)
Voodoo charms, potions and artifacts from the occult are arranged in these suitably dark rooms. Voodoo tours are available.

New Orleans Pharmacy Museum

(514 Chartres Street; open Tues-Sun 10am-5pm; ☎ 565-8027)
Founded in 1950, this museum offers a glimpse into the world of 19C medicine, through the displays of old apothecary bottles, pill tiles, powders and concoctions. Do not miss the black and rose Italian marble soda fountain (1855).

Germaine Wells Mardi Gras Museum

(Arnaud's, 813 Bienville St; opens with restaurant; ☎ 523-5433)
Set in Arnaud's restaurant, displays Carnival costumes from the daughter of the first owner, who was queen at 22 Mardi Gras balls.

Gallier House★

(1118-1132 Royal Street; open
Mon-Fri 10am-3.30pm;
☎ 525-5661)

This restored, fully furnished
Victorian house-museum was once
inhabited by prominent architect
James Gallier, who built it in 1857.
It is one of the best restored house
museums in the city, and includes
such furnishing from the period as
a working bathroom. There are
also historical exhibits, a gift shop
and a café.

Beauregard-Keyes House★

(1113 Chartres Street; open Mon-
Sat 10am-3pm; ☎ 523-7257)

This restored 19C 'raised cottage',
with its beautiful garden, was originally built in 1826 by Joseph Le
Carpentier, and consequently the
house is sometimes referred to as
the Le Carpentier House. In 1865,
Confederate General PGT Beaure-
gard rented rooms here for 18
months. Years later, novelist
Frances Parkinson Keyes lived here
and wrote prolifically. Guides in
antebellum costume
conduct tours round the
house and the pretty walled
garden.

CENTRAL BUSINESS DISTRICT
Aquarium of the Americas★★

(1 Canal Street; open daily
9.30am-6pm (Fri-Sat 7pm);
☎ 861-2537)

Opened in 1990, the
aquarium has a one
million-gallon tank holding
an impressive collection of
over 10 000 fish from
North, Central and South
America. There are five
main exhibits, showing the
animals in their environ-
mental habitats, such as the
Amazon Rainforest, the
Caribbean Reef and the
Mississippi River and Delta.

*One of the beautifully
restored rooms in the
Victorian Gallier House.*

The Aquarium of the Americas.

The Aquarium also features a large IMAX theater and space for temporary exhibitions.

WAREHOUSE DISTRICT
Louisiana Children's Museum
(420 Julia Street; open Tues-Sat 9.30am- 4.30pm, Sun noon-4.30pm. Mon 9.30am-4.30pm summer only; ☎ 523-1357)
There are plenty of hands-on exhibits here which teach children about the arts, commerce, science and industry, with an eye towards future careers, while at the same time providing hours of fun.

The museum includes the Times-Picayune Theater, which hosts a varied programme of performances, plays and puppet shows.

Confederate Museum★
(929 Camp Street; open Mon-Sat 10am-4pm; ☎ 523-4522)
The state's oldest museum, established in 1899, is devoted to the Civil War period when Louisiana seceded from the US to rally behind the Southern cause. Displays include historical documents, battle flags, uniforms, weapons and the personal effects of Confederate President Jefferson Davis.

National D-Day Museum★★
(945 Magazine Street, entrance on Andrew Higgins Drive; open daily 9am-5pm, except Thanksgiving, Christmas, New Year's Day and Mardi Gras; ☎ 527-6012)
Opened in June 2000, this museum pays tribute to the American men and women who fought World War II, both at home and in the theatres of battle. Photographs, rare film footage and wartime artifacts combine to create moving displays of the events leading up to the Allied invasions of occupied France on 6 June 1944.

MID-CITY
New Orleans Museum of Art★
(Lylong Avenue, City Park; open Tues-Sun 10am-5pm; ☎ 488-2631)
NOMA's permanent collections include American and European masters, pre-Columbian and African material, and numerous local works. The French Impressionist Edgar Degas, who often visited the city, is represented by the portrait of *Estelle Musson*. The Fabergé exhibit includes some of the Russian master jeweler's fabulous creations. The museum also houses international exhibitions and local special exhibits.

ALGIERS
Blaine Kern's Mardi Gras World
(233 Newton Street, Algiers, via

Canal Street ferry; guided tours daily 9.30am-4.30pm; ☎ 361-7821) In a vast warehouse across the river, float-builder Blaine Kern has acres of his fanciful creations on display, in various states of construction. There is a Mardi Gras gift shop and small cinema.

RIVERTOWN

In suburban Kenner, near New Orleans International Airport, several small museums are clustered together in the renovated neighborhood known as Rivertown. A multi-museum ticket is good value if you intend to visit several museums.

Louisiana Wildlife and Fisheries Museum

(303 Williams Bvd; ☎ 468-7231) This includes live fish, stuffed animals and a wealth of information about both, along with Native American craft demonstrations by members of Louisiana tribes.

Louisiana Toy Train Museum

(519 Williams Bvd; ☎ 468-7231) This former depot now honors the glory days of rail travel, and also displays some prized miniatures, with several working train layouts.

Mardi Gras Museum of Jefferson Parish

(415 Williams Bvd; ☎ 468-7231) There are simulated Mardi Gras parades here, for those who miss the real thing, along with various artifacts and films of Carnivals past.

Saints Hall of Fame Museum

(415 Williams Bvd; ☎ 468-7231) Football fans, especially followers of the Saints, will revel in the memorabilia and film-clips of this team that has yet to win a championship.

Display of heads in the Mardi Gras Museum, Rivertown.

GUIDED WALKING TOURS

While New Orleans is an ideal town for aimless exploration, guided tours with qualified companies will give you an informed perspective on the city's wealth of sites. Be aware that some hotel staff and cab drivers may be biased in their suggested tours. Use guide books or the telephone yellow pages for objective information.

Friends of the Cabildo (☎ 523-3939) provide 2-hour walking tours of the French Quarter, including most of the area's main historic buildings and entrance to several Louisiana State Museum buildings (starts in front of the 1850 House at 523 St Ann Street; Tues-Sun 10am and 1.30pm; Mon 1.30pm only).

Jean Lafitte National Historical Park and Preserve Visitor Center (☎ 589-2636), in the French Quarter, offers excellent ranger-led tours of the French Quarter, departing from the Visitor Center at 419 Decatur Street (daily 10.30am; first-come first-served; tickets available at 9am; free).

Historic New Orleans Walking Tours (☎ 947-2120) illuminates St Louis Cemetery No 1 and such voodoo sites as Congo Square, Our Lady of Guadelupe Church, the New Orleans Voodoo Spiritual Temple, and the former site of the house where the voodoo Queen Marie Laveau lived, along with her daughter, also Marie Laveau, who succeeded her (*see* p.24). They also run a Garden District Cemetery Tour.

Save Our Cemeteries (☎ 525-3377) specialize in such historic graveyards as St

Louis No 1 and Lafayette, in the Garden District.

Le Monde Creole (☎ 568-1801) gives tours of French Quarter Courtyards, conducted in both French and English.

Le'ob's Tours (☎ 288-3478) concentrates on New Orleans' African-American Heritage.

Heritage Tours (☎ 949-9805) specialize in literary tours of the French Quarter, pointing out the haunts and homes of famous artists and writers, such as Tennessee Williams, John Dos Passos, William Faulkner, and many more.

Magic Walking Tours (☎ 588-9693) offer a range of guided walking tours of St Louis Cemetery No 1, the French Quarter, the Garden District, and several 'themed' tours, including 'The Voodoo Tour' and 'The Haunted House, Vampire and Ghost-Hunt Walking Tour'.

Discover the rich wildlife of the swamps and bayous on a swamp tour.

Alligators are one of the inhabitants of the swamplands, though they are also found in the bayous within the city limits.

Swamp tours or the canoe tour at Barataria Preserve bring alligators up close – but not too close!

RIVER AND SWAMP TOURS

Numerous companies offer tours, ranging from gentle trips round the harbor, along the Mississippi, round the bayous or, more adventurously, extending into the furthest extremes of the huge areas of swampland, where you will see a variety of wildlife ranging from alligators, bald eagles, otters and beavers to maybe even black bears. Check at the tourist information office for full details, to find one that suits your needs. **Jean Lafitte National Historical Park and Preserve, Barataria Unit** (6588 Barataria Bvd, Marrero, La; ☎ 589-2330) has routes set out along boardwalks, where you can see the wildlife first hand (*see* p.72).

New Orleans Paddlewheels (☎ 529-4567) offers tours of the harbor and to Chalmette Battlefield aboard the paddlewheeler *Creole Queen* (board at Riverwalk) and the riverboat *Cajun Queen* (board at Aquarium of the Americas), as well as evening jazz cruises.

Natchez Steamboat (☎ 586-8777) offers 2-hour harbor cruises and dinner/jazz cruises on this authentic sternwheel steamboat.

Honey Island Swamp Tours (☎ 641-1769) specialize in tours to this vast, protected wetland area, led by naturalists.

Lil Cajun Swamp Tours (☎ 689-3213) provide 2-hour tours of the New Orleans' bayous.

The steamboat Natchez *sets off up the Mississippi.*

EXCURSIONS FROM NEW ORLEANS

Day Trips

It would be a shame to visit New Orleans without also taking in some of the glorious countryside, escaping temporarily from the often frantic pace of the city.

Thrills and spills with a Cajun accent await at **Jazzland★**, a New Orleans-themed amusement park just a 20-minute drive from downtown in the eastern part of the city. Water rides, rollercoasters, carousels, kiddie rides and other theme-park fare are supplemented by live music performances and a water-ski show at 'Pontchartrain Beach' (☎ 253-8000).

The **Jean Lafitte National Historical Park and Preserve, Barataria Unit** is just a 45-minute drive away, on the other side of the

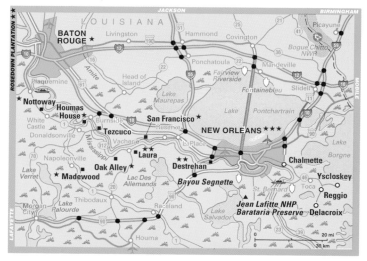

Some of the wildlife on view along the Coquille Trail boardwalk.

river, but it is truly another world. Take a hike on the **Coquille Trail** boardwalk, and stop for a moment to take in the silence and then let the subtle sounds of the swamp introduce themselves. A rich variety of wildlife may be seen on this walk, including alligators, nutria and egrets. The Park is also a fine place for canoeing. For good Cajun food on the way back to town, try **Restaurant Des Familles**.

Another great day-trip on the West Bank is to **Bayou Segnette State Park**, for boating, hiking, fishing or simple relaxation; this can be stretched into a longer break by renting a cabin with a huge screen porch, then just sitting back and doing *nothing*. On the way back to town, stop to eat at **Mosca's**.

For a different type of day-trip, accessible by car only, head downriver from the French

Map showing the area around New Orleans.

Quarter on St Claude Avenue. After crossing the bridge over the Industrial Canal, turn left at the light at Caffin Avenue and go one block to Marais Street, where you will find **Fats Domino**'s house. Nearby, next to the levee at Egania and Douglas, are the **Beaded Mansions** – two stunning steamboat Gothic houses, built by 19C river pilots of the Dollout family. One is occasionally open for tours. This, unfortunately, is not a safe area, so do not take an extended stroll.

Instead, return to St Claude and continue on to **Chalmette Battlefield★** (St Bernard Highway) where Andrew Jackson and Jean Lafitte became celebrities in 1815. On this historic site of the last battle between Great Britain and the US, Major General Sir Edward Packenham faced Jackson and his Volunteers and Lafitte and his pirates. There

The Beaded Mansions get their name from the large strings of wooden beads which decorate these two steamboat houses.

Chalmette Battlefield was the site of the famous Battle of New Orleans, in 1815.

is not a lot to see, but you can wander round the battlefield and cemeteries, or take one of the ranger talks offered by the **Chalmette Unit of the Jean Lafitte National Historical Park and Preserve** (8606 W St Bernard Highway, Chalmette, La; ☎ 281-0510).

A few miles down the road, is the **Los Isleños Museum** (1357 Bayou Road, St Bernard, La; ☎ 682-0862), a living museum devoted to this most unique of Louisiana cultures – an enclave descended from 18C émigrés from the Canary Islands, who have preserved both their Spanish dialect and folk music. Continue on into the salt-marshes and the rustic fishing villages of **Reggio**, **Ycloskey** and **Delacroix** (the latter immortalized in the Bob Dylan song *Tangled Up In Blue*). Turn around at the end of the road, and as you head back, stop for a bite at **Rocky and Carlo's**, one of New Orleans' classic blue-collar restaurants.

The Plantations★★

The **Great River Road plantations** between New Orleans and Baton Rouge are beautiful examples of architecture, although some visitors are rightfully offended that the accompanying legacy of slavery tends to be glossed over by tour guides. The houses are impressive, nonetheless, and a day trip can be made, driving up one side of the river and returning on the other. If you do not wish to drive, there are several companies offering tours of the areas. (Be forewarned, however, that bucolic landscape may suddenly give way to noxious refineries and petro-chemical plants.)

There are more palatial homes on the east bank. **Destrehan★★** is a French colonial-style house built in 1787, and reputedly home to a family of ghosts. The steamboat Gothic **San Francisco★**, near Reserve, was built in 1856, long before a scenery-spoiling refinery was stuck in the backyard. Looking at the structure of the house, with its broad galleries resembling a ship's decks and the twin stairs leading to the main portal, you can see why it is described as 'steamboat Gothic'. **Tezcuco**, near the Sunshine Bridge, south of Donaldsonville, is a lovely raised cottage, which also offers overnight accommodations. The stunning **Houmas House★**, in Burnside, is a Greek Revival showpiece. Actually, it comprises two houses, for the Greek Revival house was built in front of the original dwelling. It has magnificent gardens, and it has been used as the set for films, including *Hush Hush, Sweet Charlotte*, starring Bette Davis. Costumed guides conduct tours of the house and garden. For good local food on the east side of the river, go to **The Cabin**, in Burnside.

On the west bank of the Mississippi are two of the most famous plantation homes. **Nottoway★**, in White Castle, is one of the

Nottoway, the largest plantation home in the South, was built in 1859.

most palatial, combining Greek Revival with Italianate touches to enliven its 64 rooms. The lovely White Ballroom has splendid Corinthian columns and magnificent original chandeliers. Food and accommodations are available.

Down Louisiana Highway 18, heading back towards New Orleans, is **Oak Alley★**, in Vacherie, with its impressive alley of 28 huge live oak trees. The house, built in 1839, fell into disrepair but was lovingly restored by the Stewart family. Nearby stands **Laura**

This corridor of 300-year-old live oak trees leading up to Oak Alley has provided a romantic setting for many a film.

Inside, Oak Alley has been lovingly restored to its former glory.

Plantation★★, a colorfully-painted raised Creole cottage currently undergoing restoration. Guided tours illuminate Creole life and culture by recounting the story of the Du Parc and Locoul families, who ran the sugarcane plantation for 84 years.

Lafayette and Cajun Country★

The Cajun country around Lafayette can be visited as a day trip from New Orleans, but several leisurely days will be much more enjoyable. You can head straight out on Interstate 10 and arrive in a couple of hours, but if time allows, take the back way. Cross the Mississippi River via the **Plaquemines ferry** on Louisiana Route 75, drive through the old-time river town of Plaquemines, and then proceed along the winding, bayou-side Route 77, returning to Interstate 10 at **Grosse Tete**. Alternatively, make your way through the Fellini-like oil-industry

Enjoying the Cajun music.

graveyards around rough and tumble **Morgan City** – where huge derricks lie on their sides, rusting into oblivion – and then cruise through the sugar-cane fields around New Iberia.

Whatever your route, arriving in **Lafayette★** may be startling. At first sight, it appears to be nothing more than a fast-food strip, or at best a Southern sun-belt boom town. It is not romantic images which make this region so special, however, but the healthy balance of American mass-culture, ethnic pride and a large community of French-speaking émigrés from Europe and

Canada, many of whom teach at area schools or the University of Southwestern Louisiana. Cultural preservation is easy enough in the absence of choices but, as is the case with New Orleans, Lafayette revels in its culture and its language, despite having unlimited access to the outside world.

Musical musts in this region are discussed elsewhere (*see* p.101), but other sites are equally as important. Lafayette's lively visual arts scene is evident at the **Artists Alliance Gallery**, while zydeco-inspired painter Francis Pavy welcomes visitors to his studio. **Vermilionville★** and **Acadian Village★** are recreations of 19C Cajun villages, and offer a variety of musical and cultural programs. In the rural town of **St Martinville**, the **Evangeline Oak** is allegedly the site of the romantic tragedy chronicled by poet Longfellow; several elderly Cajun musicians can often be found socializing under the tree, on the bank of the Bayou Teche. St Martinville is a beautiful town, settled by 18C French immigrants before the Cajuns arrived from Canada. There is a striking assortment of 19C buildings around St Martins Square, and several zydeco clubs on the south side of town.

The vast swamp known as the **Atchafalaya Basin** can be explored by guided tour boats or solo canoes from McGee's Landing, on the levee road south of Henderson. In Henderson, you will find good Cajun restaurants such as **Robin's**. Other great restaurants around Cajun-Creole country include **Joe's**, in Livonia, **Mama's Fried Chicken**, in Eunice, known for its seafood rather than its poultry, and the remote, rural crawfish haven known as **Hawk's**, outside of Rayne.

The Atchafalaya Basin swamps are the third largest swamps in the US.

Once refreshed, resume exploring. **Jungle Gardens★** (south of New Iberia) is a horticultural extravaganza, an eccentric assemblage of plants and statuary from around the world. Built by the McIlhenny family, who manufacture Tabasco on nearby Avery Island, it is a fascinating place to spend a day. On a smaller scale is **Jefferson Island** (not actually an island, but a lake created from the collapse of an underground salt mine), where the manicured, geometric gardens bloom with azaleas and camellias in spring.

WEATHER

For a good part of the year – approximately May to October – New Orleans is consistently hot and humid. Damp and humid conditions are also frequent in winter, but are often accompanied by a penetrating chill. Temperatures rarely dip below freezing though, and then only briefly, but many winter visitors come unprepared, with no heavy coat or sweaters. The most pleasant, temperate, low-humidity months are October, November, February and early March, but by late April the heat has usually returned.

Those who have never experienced such sub-tropical conditions find it hard to imagine how debilitating they can be. Always wear a hat, if you must be outdoors in such weather, and drink plenty of liquids. Applying sun screen is also a good idea.

Many summer afternoons are climaxed by thunderstorms; experienced travelers book early-morning flights to avoid the likelihood of rough weather. Rain is frequent in New Orleans, and can be quite intense. Should you be in town when the arrival of a hurricane is announced, leave as soon as possible; there is nothing adventurous about riding out such a catastrophe, and the city may be cut off for many days afterward.

CALENDAR OF EVENTS

January: The **Sugar Bowl** is a college football classic, held at the Superdome; Jan 8: **Battle of New Orleans commemorative events** at the Chalmette Battlefield.
February: The dates of **Mardi Gras** vary, but with the exception of 4 March 2003 it will

fall in February through to the year 2010.

March: The Crescent City Classic, a 16 mile (10km) race for joggers and walkers; **St Patrick's Day** festivities, followed by **St Joseph's Day**, an important holiday for both the Italian community and the Mardi Gras Indians.

April: The French Quarter Festival; **Festival Internationale de La Louisiane** in Lafayette; and the first week of the **New Orleans Jazz and Heritage Festival** (**Jazzfest**), held at the Fair Grounds Race Track.

May: The Greek Festival; second week of **Jazzfest**.

June: The **Great French Market Tomato**

The Crescent City Classic, beginning at Jackson Square and ending at Audubon Park, attracts top international runners.

Festival in the French Market; **Carnival Latino**, Riverfront; **Reggae Riddums Festival** in City Park.

July: **Go Fourth on the River festivities and fireworks** on the Riverfront.

August: **Zydeco Festival** in Plaisance.

September: **Festivals Acadiens** in Lafayette; the **Louisiana Folklife Festival** in the city of Monroe, in north-eastern Louisiana.

October: **Swamp Fest** at Audubon Zoo; **Oktoberfest** at the Deutsches Haus; **Jazz Awareness Month**, with daily performances and lectures. Numerous rural festivals.

November: **Thanksgiving**; **(Nov-Dec) Celebration in the Oaks** sound and light show opens at City Park.

December: **Christmas caroling** in Jackson Square; Christmas eve **bonfires** on the levee between New Orleans and Baton Rouge; **New Year's Eve** countdown in Jackson Square.

ACCOMMODATIONS

New Orleans is full of intriguing, atmospheric places to stay. Most hotels are found in the French Quarter and Central Business District (frequented by businessmen), but there are some stately hotels in the Garden District. Almost all hotels have air conditioning, and most larger ones have swimming pools. Although New Orleans boasts over 30 000 hotel rooms, booking is necessary well in advance during Mardi Gras and Jazzfest (when prices may also go up).

Prices in general vary considerably, but there is something to suit all tastes and pockets. The most expensive hotels will charge $125 or more per night, while moderate-priced lodgings can be found for $60-100. There are also innumerable guest houses, some offering very reasonably-priced accommodations, together with motels and bed and breakfast accommodations at $50 or less. B&B can be booked on www.LouisianaBandB.com.

The Longpré Guest House 1726 Prytania Street, New Orleans, LA 70130 (☎ 581-4540) offers Garden District accommodations at $12 per person per night. Information on hostels can be found in the *International Youth Hostel Handbook*, available from the Youth Hostels Association.

Recommendations

To thoroughly experience the real New Orleans, avoid staying in a generic national-chain hotel and instead book a room at an establishment with authentic, romantic local flavor. The **Melrose Mansion** (937 Esplanade Ave, ☎ 944-2255) is the ultimate in luxury, situated in an elegant Victorian mansion (very expensive). Sister hotels include the **River Inn** (1011 Esplanade) and **Girod House** (835 Esplanade). The **Pontchartrain Hotel** (2031 St Charles Ave, ☎ 524-0581) is 25 minutes' walk from the French Quarter, and features the well-known Caribbean Room Restaurant (very expensive). The **Columns Hotel** (3811 St Charles Ave, ☎ 899-9308), situated in the heart of Uptown, offers live jazz on its lovely front porch, plus elegant bed-and-breakfast accommodations (fairly expensive). Slightly cheaper is the **ParkView Guest House** (7004 St Charles Ave, ☎ 861-7564), furnished with antiques, offering a taste of the past, with some rooms overlooking Audubon Park (fairly expensive).

For moderate lodging, the **Mazant Street Guest House** (☎ 944-2662) and the **Dusty Mansion** (☎ 895-4576) are both economical and appeal to a younger/international,

casual crowd. Other no-frills options include
The Hummingbird (804 St Charles Ave,
☎ 523-9165, 561-9229), the **La Salle Hotel**
(1113 Canal St, ☎ 523-5831, 800-521-9450),
and the **London Lodge** (9301 Airline
Highway, ☎ 488-8767).

FOOD AND DRINK

New Orleans is one of the world's great food
destinations, from the smartest white-linen
establishments to the greasiest corner dives.
It is also a town that is not afraid of robust
seasoning, although the recent Louisiana
food fad has inspired indiscriminate
cayenne overkill in some circles; the highly-
touted 'blackened' dishes so avidly
consumed by tourists were a passing fad,
rarely served at local family gatherings.

Since many dishes are unique to New
Orleans and the surrounding countryside, a
brief glossary may make local menus
comprehensible. **Andouille**
is a Cajun pork sausage,
often served with the classic
dish of **red beans and rice**.
Dirty rice is white rice with
ground meat or giblets,
served as a side dish or as
dressing for poultry.
Jambalaya is also a rice
concoction, with large
chunks of sausage, chicken,
and/or seafood, and usually
considered a main course.
Gumbo is a thick, stew-like
soup brimming with
shellfish, chicken, sausage
and okra, and often
seasoned with ground
sassafras or *filé*;

*Morning fare –
the lavish breakfast
at Brennan's
(below) or simple
café au lait and
beignets at Café du
Monde. For a
musical wake-up,
try the jazz brunch
at Commander's
Palace or the
Sunday gospel
brunch at the
House of Blues.*

courtbouillon is even thicker, and features fish, particularly catfish, in a tomato-based sauce. A **muffuletta** is a large Italian sandwich filled with miscellaneous antipasto and served on a round bun, while a **po' boy** (slang for *poor boy*) is a sandwich served on crusty French bread and filled with fried seafood, ham and cheese, or roast beef in thick gravy. **Meunière** is a sauce used for serving fish, usually sea trout, by dusting it in flour and sautéing it in butter, while **remoulade** is a sauce of olive oil, mustard, horseradish and various spices, and served over chilled shrimp.

Recommendations

Visitors to New Orleans are often struck by the time and passion, bordering on obsession, that locals devote to discussing and enjoying the relative merits of favorite restaurants. While recommendations are subjective, of course, the following restaurants all command fiercely loyal local followings.

The French Quarter

Galatoire's *209 Bourbon St* ☎ 525-2021
Perhaps the best of the old-line institutions for classic New Orleans cuisine. Don't miss the *oysters en brochette.*

Antoine's *713 St Louis St* ☎ 581-4422
A venerable Creole restaurant, popular with old New Orleans families. Steaks, oysters, and for dessert, the towering baked Alaska.

Arnaud's *813 Bienville St* ☎ 523-5433 Faultless service and exquisite decor match the expertly prepared Creole cuisine.

Brennan's *417 Royal St* ☎ 525-9711 Lavish breakfasts (try the *Eggs Sardou*) in plush rooms or on the romantic patio.

K-Paul's Louisiana Kitchen *416 Chartres St*

☎ 524-7394 Chef Paul Prudhomme pioneered the revival of Cajun cuisine from this pleasant, rustic restaurant.

NOLA *534 St Louis St* ☎ 522-6652 Contemporary Louisiana cuisine in a trendy setting, all courtesy of celebrity chef Emeril Lagasse.

The Pelican Club *312 Exchange Alley* ☎ 523-1504 Intriguing cuisine, blending Louisiana, Asian and International influences.

Bayona *430 Dauphine St* ☎ 525-4455 Chef Susan Spicer creates innovative contemporary American dishes in a romantic, comfortable setting.

Peristyle *1041 Dumaine St* ☎ 593-9535 Classy, updated bistro serves forth outstanding American food with Louisiana and French influences.

Acme Oyster House *724 Iberville St* ☎ 522-5973 Delectable raw oysters are the specialty

Antoine's restaurant, on St Louis Street, serves classic Creole dishes in traditional surroundings.

at this fun, workaday joint.

Napoleon House *500 Chartres St* ☎ 524-9752
Munch on tasty bar food, listen to opera, and watch the crowds go by at this atmospheric, old-time watering hole.

Central Grocery *923 Decatur St* ☎ 523-1620
Originator of the muffaletta sandwich, this ethnic Italian grocery and lunch bar is redolent of olives and spices.

Bella Luna *914 N Peters St* ☎ 529-1583
Continental cuisine with Italian influences, in a romantic spot overlooking the river.

Louis XVI *730 Bienville St* ☎ 581-7000 Classic French cuisine in sumptuous surroundings.

Le Croissant d'Or *617 Ursulines St* ☎ 524-4663 Authentic French pastry shop serving breakfast and lunch.

House of Blues *225 Decatur St* ☎ 529-2583
Down-home Southern food accompanies great live music; go for the Sunday-morning gospel brunch.

Mother's, on Poydras Street, where some say you'll find the best po' boys in town.

Central Business District

Mother's *401 Poydras St* ☎ 523-9656 A no-frills favorite for po' boys, jambalaya and gargantuan lunch platters.

Grill Room *300 Granvier St* ☎ 522-1992 Exquisitely innovative cuisine in a supremely elegant setting within the Windsor Court Hotel.

Sazerac *123 Baronne St* ☎ 529-4773 Plush surroundings in the Fairmont Hotel, with Continental-French cuisine.

Palace Café *605 Canal St* ☎ 523-1661 Outstanding Cajun-Creole food in a former music store; don't miss the white chocolate bread pudding.

Bon Ton Café *401 Magazine St* ☎ 524-3386 Heady Cajun and Creole dishes in a prosaic, workaday setting favored by the office crowd.

Smith & Wollensky *1009 Poydras St* ☎ 561-0770 Classic steakhouse fare and giant martinis in a lovely, historic building.

Warehouse District

Herbsaint *701 St Charles Ave* ☎ 524-4114 A new arrival by chef Susan Spicer, featuring French-American bistro food with a Southern twist.

Emeril's *800 Tchoupitoulas St* ☎ 528-9393 Flagship restaurant of celebrity chef Emeril Lagasse features innovative, Creole-American food in a hip, lively atmosphere.

Taqueria Corona *857 Fulton St* ☎ 524-9805 Authentic Mexican food at very reasonable prices; try the delicious soft tacos.

The Red Bike *746 Tchoupitoulas St* ☎ 529-2453 Salads and wholegrain items are a vegetarian's delight.

Malute's *201 Julia St* ☎ 522-1492 Rural Cajun food accompanies the Cajun bands that play nightly, to enthusiastic dancing.

Garden District

Commander's Palace *1403 Washington Ave*
☎ 899-8221 Acknowledged as one of the
finest restaurants in the city; classic New
Orleans cuisine includes turtle soup, fish
dishes and sinful desserts, all accompanied
by excellent service.

Parasol's *2533 Constance St* ☎ 899-2054
Atmospheric little po' boy shop that serves
as the center for St Patrick's Day festivities,
green beer and all.

Café Atchafalaya *901 Louisiana Ave* ☎ 891-
5271 Noted for fried green tomatoes and
other Southern home-cooking delicacies.

Uglesich's *1238 Baronne St* ☎ 523-8571
Exquisite food, especially barbecue shrimp,
is not to be missed, although the
neighbourhood is dicey.

Delmonico *1300 St Charles Ave* ☎ 525-4937
Emeril Lagasse's newest New Orleans
venture, serving American cuisine with a
Creole accent.

Uptown

Bluebird Café *3625 Prytania St* ☎ 895-7166
Popular, moderately-priced bohemian
hangout serving breakfast until 3pm.

Casamento's *4330 Magazine St* ☎ 895-9761
Oysters raw and fried are the specialty at this
unique institution, decorated floor-to-ceiling
with colourful tiles.

Camellia Grill *626 Carrollton Ave* ☎ 866-9573
Famed for chili-cheese omelettes, delicious
hamburgers and the snappy patter of the
counter-men.

Brigsten's *723 Dante St* ☎ 861-7610 A rising
star on the culinary map; Cajun-inspired
cuisine in a comfortable old cottage.

Kelsey's *3923 Magazine St* ☎ 897-6722
Inspired Cajun-Creole dishes in the heart of

Magazine Street's gallery district.

Upperline *1413 Upperline St* ☎ 891-9822
Haute Creole fare in a decorative, fine-art setting.

Zachary's *8400 Oak St* ☎ 865-1559 Creole soul food will warm your hear in the cozy renovated cottage.

La Crêpe Nanou *1410 Robert St* ☎ 899-2670 Authentic Gallic cuisine; don't miss the steamed mussels.

Dick & Jenny's *4501 Tchoupitoulas St* ☎ 894-9880 French Creole specialties in a homey renovated cottage.

Mid-City

Mandina's *3800 Canal St* ☎ 482-9179 Great shrimp remoulade and trout meunière; don't mind the surly waiters.

Luizza's *3636 Bienville St* ☎ 482 9120 Cajun-Creole and Italian in a raucous, blue-collar environment.

Royal Street boasts some of the city's most exclusive antique shops.

Benna-Chin *133 N Carrollton Ave* ☎ 486-1313 West African cuisine emphasizes New Orleans' Afro-Caribbean connections.
Garce's *4200 D'Hemecourt St* ☎ 488-4734 Cuban restaurant known for pork with yucca and delicious mango milkshakes.

SHOPPING

The three most unique shopping districts in New Orleans are the French Quarter, Magazine Street, and Riverbend.

   The French Quarter is also rife with souvenir and T-shirt shops that have become a blemish on the neighborhood and need no endorsement here. The upper end of the Quarter, along Chartres and Royal Streets, is a world-famous center for the **antique** trade, and the home of such renowned showrooms as **M S Rau Inc** (630 Royal St), **Rothschild's** (241 Royal St) and **Waldhorn & Adler** (343 Royal St). These establishments deal in major *objets d'art* rather than amusing, moderately-priced knick-knacks. The latter are more likely to be found in the lower end of the Quarter, near Esplanade Avenue.

   Kruz (432 Barracks St) is an ethnic boutique, specializing in clothing from around the world, while **A Fair Approach** (824 Chartres St) bypasses the middleman to bring unique handcrafted items from Third World countries directly to clients. An eclectic mix of handcrafted items made by Louisiana artists is on sale at **Crafty Louisianians** (813 Royal St), while works of a more classical nature are available at **Kurt E Schon Ltd** (523 Royal St). The **Gallery For Fine Photography** (322 Royal St) lives up to its name, though it is not inexpensive.

   Recommended bookstores include **Faulkner House Books** (624 Pirates Alley),

Beckam's Bookshop (228 Decatur St) and **The Librairie** (823 Chartres). For delicious gift packages of local delicacies try the **Café du Monde Gift Shop** (813 Decatur St) and remember that fresh seafood in special packaging is available at the airport.

Handmade Mardi Gras masks are a uniquely New Orleanian item, made on-site and sold at **Little Shop of Fantasy** (523 Dumaine St) and at **Maskarade** (630 St Ann St). Locally-made perfumes fill the air at **Hove Parfumeur Ltd** (824 Royal St). To take home some great Louisiana music, **Rock and Roll Collectibles** (1214 Decatur St) deals in secondhand records, while **Louisiana Music Factory** (210 Decatur St) has an extensive range of new CDs. The **Virgin Records Megastore** also has an outstanding selection of music by local artists.

Magazine Street, from Magazine Row all the way up to Nashville Avenue, is known more for affordable **antiques** than those on Royal, as well as for a fine selection of pottery, jewelry, and other crafted items. **Mario Villa** (3908 Magazine St) displays Villa's unique furniture, along with miscellaneous sculpture, photography, and more; **Casey Willems Pottery** (3919 Magazine St) is as reasonably priced as it is

Magazine Street is noted for its antique shops – but remember, you will have to transport your purchases home!

The Esplanade shopping mall.

lovely and functional. **Didier Inc** (3439 Magazine St) specializes in American furniture, as does **Dodge-Fjeld Antiques** (2033 Magazine St). If the many stores create a bewildering choice, antiques consultant **Macon Riddle** may be able to advise you.

Riverbend is the home base of custom jeweler **Mignon Faget Ltd** (718 Dublin St), custom clothier **Yvonne LaFleur** (8131 Hampson St) and the excellent children's store **Kid's Stuff** (714 Dublin St). **The Sun Shop** (7722 Maple St) will brighten your day with Central American clothing and pottery. Improve your mind at **The Maple Street Bookshop** (7523 Maple St), and then indulge yourself with some fine pastry at **La Bonbonnière** (1114 S Carrollton).

For more generic items, the following shopping centers are also recommended: the New Orleans Center, Uptown Square, Canal Place, Jax Brewery, the Riverwalk, Lakeside Mall and Esplanade Mall.

New Orleans' best-known thoroughfare, Bourbon Street, is packed with bars of all descriptions.

ENTERTAINMENT AND NIGHTLIFE

Live music is one of New Orleans' strongest attractions, and few cities anywhere in the world can claim a comparable music scene. There is some debate about the city's status as the literal birthplace of jazz, but some of its earliest and most important evolution occurred in New Orleans. Such growth has continued ever since, with an important resurgence during the past 15 years.

Information on musical events, the latest clubs, and so on is available from the **Louisiana Jazz Federation** (☎ 364-5995), or from the knowledgeable staff at the **Louisiana Music Factory** record store (☎ 586-1094). The New Orleans' daily newspaper, *The Times-Picayune,* has an entertainment section called *Lagniappe* in its Friday edition. Music listings are also available in the monthly magazines *Offbeat* and *New Orleans,* and *Gambit Weekly,* which

Experience New Orleans tradition with a dose of hot Dixieland jazz at Preservation Hall. Fork over a ten-spot and the veteran musicians will play 'When the Saints Go Marching In'...

appears on Mondays. New Orleans' community radio station, WWOZ (90.7 FM), broadcasts a daily events update.

Jazz

Contemporary New Orleans has preserved few traces of the early jazz scene, because its significance was not appreciated at the time, nearly a century ago. Yet two French Quarter venues, **Preservation Hall** and the **Palm Court Jazz Café**, are committed to presenting New Orleans jazz in the most traditional form possible. Preservation Hall is by far the best known of the two, but its spartan comforts – no chairs, no bar – hardly encourage a long stay. The Palm Court, in contrast, offers the same fine music in a pleasant supper-club setting.

Jazz can also be heard on the streets of the

Energy and enthusiasm are in plentiful supply in the street parades.

New Orleans jazz at Maison Bourbon.

French Quarter, especially in Jackson Square, Latrobe Park and at the corner of St Peter and Royal, on days when the street is closed to cars. The styles played range from strictly traditional to the modern young brass bands, whose members have blended New Orleans' venerable repertoire with such contemporary influences as funk, rap and hip-hop. These groups can be heard nightly at **Donna's Bar & Grill**, and at various clubs across Rampart Street, in an historic but rough section known as **Tremé**. Brass bands also play in the streets during jazz funerals, 'second line' parades, and other community functions.

Some purists in traditional New Orleans jazz regard the related genre of Dixieland as a lame imitation of the real thing. It remains popular, however, and can be heard at nightclubs including **Pete Fountain's**, the **Famous Door**, the **Tin Roof Café**, **Maison**

Bourbon, and at Sunday brunches at **Le Jardin**, **Commander's Palace** and **Arnaud's**.

New Orleans is also home to an impressive modern jazz scene that has produced such nationally prominent figures as Wynton and Branford Marsalis, and Harry Connick Jr. There are some excellent spots to soak up these progressive sounds, including **Snug Harbor**, the **Funky Butt**, the **Crescent City Brewhouse**, **Storyville**, **Kemp's** and for the popular new modern-jazz, a swanky cabaret known as **The Red Room**, Uptown (for Jazzfest *see* p.104).

Rhythm & Blues

Like jazz, rhythm & blues includes many elements of African-American and European folk traditions, and contemporary popular music. R & B evolved during the late 1940s, with New Orleans firmly in the vanguard. Local heroes such as Fats Domino went on to international stardom, while stars such as Little Richard came to New Orleans to record, in the hope that local musicians could provide that elusive 'hit' quality.

Such activity took place between the late 1940s and early 1960s, which is now regarded as 'the Golden Age' of New Orleans rhythm & blues. Today, the Crescent City is still an active R & B center. Pioneering artists such as Fats Domino, Allen Toussaint, Frankie Ford and Tommy Ridgley still perform, as do 1960s and 1970s artists such as the Neville Brothers, the Meters, Johnny Adams and Snooks Eaglin. A new generation of R & B artists, represented by the likes of Davell Crawford, keeps the tradition alive. Clubs presenting live New Orleans rhythm & blues include **Tipitina's** (named for a song by R & B legend Professor Longhair), now with three separate clubs in Uptown, the

Warehouse District and the French Quarter, **Storyville**, the **Maple Leaf**, **Café Brazil**, **Snug Harbor**, **Ernie K-Doe's Mother-In-Law Lounge**, **Jimmy's**, the **Mid-City Lanes** (the 'Rock and bowl'), the **Lion's Den** (where owner Irma Thomas frequently performs), the **House of Blues**, **Howlin' Wolf**, **Treasure Chest Casino**, **Bally's Casino**, and others.

Rock Music

Rock music is also performed at many of the above clubs, as well as at the **Mermaid Lounge, Carrollton Station**, the **Rivershack, Checkpoint Charlie's, Margaritaville** and **The Live Bait**. New Orleans has an active punk-rock scene, as well, replete with green hair, tattoos, body piercing and other such accoutrements. Clubs that present punk-rock, and more recent trends, include the **Mermaid Lounge**, the **Shim Sham Club, Checkpoint Charlie's**, and **Jimmy's**.

Cajun and Zydeco

Cajun music and its black Creole

Fats Domino, perhaps one of the most famous sons of New Orleans, performs in the city.

Traditional zydeco player.

counterpart, **zydeco**, are not native to New Orleans, but originate in the countryside west of New Orleans. Once scorned as coarse, passé and rural, recent years have seen them become more fashionable, accompanied by the craze for Cajun cooking and Chef Paul Prudhomme's blackened creations. The huge success of the film *The Big Easy* also opened many opportunities for South Louisiana musicians, despite its inaccurate depiction of regional culture.

The term 'zydeco', incidentally, is an elision of the French *les haricots*, or 'the snapbeans'. There's an old Creole dance song entitled *Les haricots sont pas salés*, which literally means 'the snap beans are not salty'. This became a metaphor for hard times, when people could not afford salt or salt-pork to season their food, and the song then emerged as the name for an entire musical genre. The late Clifton Chenier pioneered contemporary zydeco; today's leading artists include Stanley 'Buckwheat' Dural, Geno Delafosse, and Nathan and the Zydeco Cha-Chas. Prominent Cajun musicians include Belton Richard, Michael Doucet and Beausoleil, the Hackberry Ramblers, and Steve Riley and the Mamou Playboys.

Both Cajun music and zydeco are sung mostly in French, are primarily played to encourage dancing, and feature the accordion as their principal instrument. Both draw on such diverse sources as country music, rock and rhythm & blues, to varying degrees, but Cajun music also draws on Acadian and French folk music, while zydeco has Afro-Caribbean folk roots, and tends to be more assertively rhythmic.

Cajun music and zydeco draw capacity crowds of happy dancers to such New Orleans nightclubs as **Michaul's**, **Mulate's**, the **Mid-City Lanes**, the **Cajun Cabin**; the **Maple Leaf**, **Tipitina's**, and the **House of Blues**. While a night dancing in New Orleans is great fun, the music is best experienced on its rural turf around Lafayette, Eunice, and Opelousas. Zydeco clubs include **Slim's Y-Ki-Ki** in Opelousas, **Richard's** in Lawtell, and **El Sido's** in Lafayette, while **Bourque's** in Lewisburg is best for Cajun music. In addition, a variety show called *Rendez-vous des Cajuns*, conducted in French and broadcast live over radio, is held every Saturday at 6pm

You'll never forget listening to live blues, R &B and zydeco while bowling down a tenpin at the Rock N' Bowl. It's a truly unique New Orleans instiution.

at the Liberty Theater in Eunice.

All of the above and more can be heard simultaneously at the **New Orleans Jazz and Heritage Festival**. Held during the last week of April and the first week of May, 'Jazzfest' has emerged as an international event on a par with Mardi Gras. The festival is held on the infield of the Fair Grounds Race Track, where 12 stages scattered across the site present a wealth of Louisiana music, with related styles from around the world. In addition, a fine selection of traditional and contemporary crafts are sold, as is regional food. Jazzfest also encompasses a series of evening concerts, held around town, and free educational workshops in the city's schools (for information ☎ 941-5100).

Classical Music and Theater

As one of the New World's first outposts of French culture and society, it is only natural that New Orleans should have a rich heritage in classical music and opera. The city even boasts an accomplished composer, Louis Moreau Gottschalk, whose 19C works combined the complexity of Chopin with Afro-Caribbean folk sources. A full schedule of annual performances is given by the **Louisiana Philharmonic Orchestra**, the **New Orleans Opera Association**, the **Jefferson Performing Arts Society**, and the theater departments of **Xavier**, **Tulane** and **Loyola Universities**. Nationally-touring musicals frequently appear at the **Saenger Theater**, while local productions of musicals and plays are held at **Le Petit Theater du Vieux Carré**, the **Southern Repertory Theater**, the **Contemporary Arts Center**, and the **Rivertown Repertory Theater**.

Casinos

Harrah's Casino, in its massive new building

The Saenger Theater has been splendidly restored and now provides an opulent setting for Broadway productions.

at the foot of Canal Street, draws thousands of gamblers every day to its New Orleans-accented games of chance. **Bally's** (1 Stars and Stripes Boulevard, South Shore Harbor; ☎ 248-3200) and **Treasure Chest** (5050 Williams Boulevard, Kenner; ☎ 443-8000) are both on Lake Pontchartrain. Across the river, in Harvey, is **The Boomtown Belle** (4132 Peters Rd; ☎ 393-6445).

SPORTS

The Crescent City's professional football team, the **New Orleans Saints**, has performed dismally in recent years and has never won a national championship, but perpetually optimistic fans still adore them. The Saints' home games are played during the fall at the **Louisiana Superdome**. College football is equally popular, and while the hometown team from **Tulane University** is undistinguished, the Tigers from **Louisiana State University**, up the road in Baton Rouge, are perennial national contenders. The European form of football, known in

The Louisiana Superdome hosts the Saints' games and other sporting events.

the US as 'soccer', is increasingly popular in New Orleans, due in large part to the city's burgeoning Central American community; games are frequently played in **Tad Gormley Stadium** in City Park. For further details check with **Club Soccer** (☎ 464-4661) or the **Lafrenière Soccer Association** (☎ 465-8224).

Despite on-going efforts to bring majo.-league baseball to New Orleans, no team yet exists, but the **New Orleans Zephyrs** draw fervent crowds while training the stars of the future. College baseball, another source of future major-leaguers, is also popular locally, thanks to fine teams at **Tulane**, the **University of New Orleans** and **Louisiana State University**. The 20 000-seat **New Orleans Arena**, located on Girod Street accross from the Superdome, hosts basketball, hockey games and concerts.

Horse-racing enjoys great popularity in the region, with racing seasons at the **Fair Grounds** and **Jefferson Downs**.

Moving from spectator sports to participation, **cycling** is easy in New Orleans' flat terrain, though riders should be wary of the city's oblivious drivers. Information on races and rallies is available from **Crescent City Cyclists**, (☎ 276-2601), while **Bicycle Michael's** (☎ 945-9505) rents equipment.

Canoeists will enjoy the 22 000 acres (8 910ha) of alligator-inhabited marsh at **Bayou Sauvage National Wildlife Refuge** (☎ 646-7544), located within the city limits. There are similar conditions at the **Barataria Unit of Jean Lafitte National Historical Park** (☎ 589-2330.) For white-water excitement, **Okatoma Canoe Rental** at Okatoma Creek near Hattiesburg, Mississippi, is well worth the 2-hour drive (☎ 601-722-4297); for quieter paddling in a wooded setting, the

Bogue Chitto River near Bush, Louisiana, is
ideal (☎ 735-1173.) The less intrepid will
enjoy boating on City Park's lovely lagoons.
Sailing on Lake Pontchartrain is popular
year round, with rentals available from **Tim
Murray Sailboats** (☎ 283-2507).

Public **golf** courses in the city include
Audubon Park; Brechtel, on the west bank;
City Park; and Joe Bartholomew. City Park
and Audubon Park also offer public **tennis**
courts. To view the local landscape on
horseback, check with Cascade Stables in
Audubon Park (☎ 891-2246) or City Park
Riding Stables (☎ 483-9398).

One of Louisiana's official slogans is
'sportsman's paradise' – a boastful yet quite
accurate description of the state's bountiful
resources for hunting and fishing, in both
fresh and salt-water. For information on
licenses and other legal requirements, check
with the **Louisiana Wildlife and Fisheries
Department** (☎ 568-5636).

*City Park provides
many leisure
activities, such
as golf.*

*With water all
around, New
Orleans has some
excellent fishing
to offer.*

THE BASICS

Note: This guide is intended for US, Canadian and overseas visitors. Some details therefore will not apply to everyone. Sections of particular reference to non-US residents are marked with an asterisk [*].

Before You Go *

British citizens planning on staying in the US as ordinary tourists for a period of up to 90 days do not need a visitor's visa. All that is required is a valid passport, and a visa waiver form, which may be obtained in advance from a travel agent, or provided by the airline during check-in. This form must be handed in to immigration on arrival. Certain categories of visitor, such as those planning to do business within the US, need a visa.

Visitors from many other parts of the world, including Eire, require a valid passport and a non-immigrant visitor's visa. Details are available from the nearest US embassy or consulate.

Vaccinations are not required.

Getting There *

Flights to New Orleans arrive at New Orleans International Airport in Kenner, 15 miles (24km) west of the city. Flights from Europe are few and far between, but there are frequent domestic flights, so you might find it best to fly to another major airport and transfer. There are, however, frequent flights from Nicaragua, El Salvador, Guatamala and Honduras.

Prices vary widely according to the season, and there are many discounts to be had. Low-cost flights can often be arranged through travel agents who specialize in long-distance flights, or by booking a charter flight. APEX or Super-APEX tickets may be bought directly from the airlines. Travel ads in the Sunday newspapers or the various listing magazines are the best places to look.

Fly-drive and flight-plus-accommodations offers can work out cheaper than booking everything separately, and brochures on these types of vacations are available from travel agents.

It is worth noting that booking your flight 21 days or more in advance of traveling can cut your fare by as much as two thirds, so it is a good idea to start planning your trip to New Orleans well before you intend to go.

Colorful Mardi Gras Indian head-dress.

A-Z

Arriving *

If you are a non-US citizen coming from outside the country, you must complete immigration and customs declaration forms during the flight, and hand them in once you land. You will be asked where you plan to spend the first night, and when you intend to leave the country. You might also be asked to prove that you can support yourself financially during your stay, and any indication that you cannot might result in admission being refused.

To expedite your progress through customs, pay special attention to Question 9 on your declaration form; this relates to fruit, plants, meats, food, soil, live animals (including birds) and farm products.

Buses are available for transportation from the airport to the Central Business District (CBD). The fares are reasonable and the service is frequent. Taxis tend to be quite expensive, with prices comparing unfavorably with those even in New York, but are good value if three or more people are traveling together. Airport Shuttle Inc. also provides an excellent service, taking you directly to your hotel (☎ 522-3500). Transportation back to the airport at the end of your stay is also available providing you give them at least a day's notice.

Accidents and Breakdowns

Check to see if your initial car rental charge includes LDW (loss damage waiver), a type of insurance that covers the car you are driving. It is not particularly cheap (between $12 and $20 a day), but without it you are liable for every bump and scratch on the car. If it does not come as part of the deal, it is worth adding it on.

An emergency telephone number will be given to you in case your rented car breaks down. Otherwise, get the car to the side of the road, lift the lid over the engine and wait for the highway patrol or state police to come by. Women driving alone are not advised to advertise the fact that they are in trouble. A mobile phone can be rented from the car agency, and will offer a lifeline in an emergency.

Accommodations see **p.86**

Airports see **Getting There, p.108**

Babysitters see **Children**

Banks

These are open weekdays, 9am-3pm or 4pm. Some stay open later on Fridays, and a few open on Saturday mornings.

Banks are probably the best places to change travelers' checks. It is advisable to bring US dollar travelers' checks (cheques), which are widely accepted like cash. Visitors from around the world have access to cash withdrawals, using major credit cards and bank cards at the automatic teller machines available at most banks. It is advisable to get lists of outlets and charges from your home bank.

Bicycles

New Orleans is a very flat city, so it is an ideal place for cycling. There are organized bike tours through the French Quarter, and the Garden District.

Outlets offering bikes for rent can be found in the Yellow Pages. There are many outlets in City Park and the French Quarter. For more information contact French Quarter Bicycles, 522 Dumaine, ☎ **529-3136**.

Books

Here are a few suggestions for reading to enhance your stay in New Orleans:

Great Houses of New Orleans,
    by Curt Bruce
*The Encyclopaedia of Cajun and
    Creole Cuisine*, by John Folse
Fabulous New Orleans,
    by Lyle Saxon
New Orleans Unmasqued,
    by S Frederick Starr
*Mardi Gras & Bacchus:
    Something Old, Something New*,
    by Myron Tassin
*Satchmo – My Life in New
Orleans*,
    by Louis Armstrong
Old Creole Days,
    by George Washington
Extreme Prejudice,
    by Frederick Barton
Pylon, by William Faulkner
Keepers of the House,
    by Shirley Ann Grau
A Confederacy of Dunces,
    by John Kennedy Toole
The Moviegoer, by Walter Percy
*Interview with the Vampire, The
    Queen of the Damned, The
    Witching Hour, The Vampire*

Lestat, by Anne Rice
Storyville, by Al Rose
Life on the Mississippi,
   by Mark Twain
A Streetcar Named Desire, A Rose Tattoo,
   by Tennessee Williams

Breakdowns see **Accidents**

Buses see **Transportation**

Car Rental *

Rental cars are widely available through airports, hotels or individual rental companies. Prices can vary a great deal, so compare prices before you book. It is a good idea to book a car well in advance if you can as this can result in considerable discounts.

The minimum rental age is 21, although some companies impose a limit of 25, and others increase insurance premiums for those under 25. You will be expected to pay by credit card, and if you don't have one a large deposit may be demanded.

Arranging fly-drive or booking a car before arriving in New Orleans can be extremely economical. Try to get free unlimited mileage, and note that there will probably be a drop-off charge for leaving the car at a different location. Scrutinize the small print of your rental agreement for mention of a loss damage waiver (LDW), and if this is not included in the price, seriously consider buying it.

See also **Accidents and Breakdowns** and **Driving**

Children

Many hotels allow children to stay in their parents' room free of charge, while others offer special children's rates. Enquire in advance whether the hotel offers a babysitting service or any special children's activities.

Babysitting services are offered by The Accent on Children's Arrangements (☎ 524-1227), Dependable Kid Care (☎ 486-4001).

New Orleans is full of fun things to keep your children occupied. It is worthwhile buying a guidebook such as *New Orleans for Kids* (which can be purchased from the Jackson Square Tourist Office). Children are welcome in many restaurants, such as Café du Monde, where the entertainers who gather in the area outside will keep them amused.

Churches see **Religion**

Climate see **p.83**

Houma Bridge at sunset.

Clothing

What to wear in New Orleans is very much dependent on when and where you are planning to go. As with the rest of the US, the overall rule is informality. At carnival times absolutely anything goes. In fact the usual dress code in the French Quarter is extremely relaxed. In summer, when it can be very humid, T-shirts and shorts are cool, practical and acceptable. In spring and fall a lightweight coat or jacket may be needed.

In winter the weather is very varied. It is advisable to take outfits which may be teamed either with shirts or with wool sweaters. Some restaurants require smarter attire, but this usually just means ties and jackets for men and no jeans or shorts. A warning though – all-year-round air conditioning lends a chill to even the less upscale eateries, so a jacket is always a good idea.

* Visitors from the UK will find that women's clothing sizes are always a size less. Men's suits and shirts are identical to UK sizes. Shoe sizes are 1-1.5 above British ones. A handy guide to the sizing differences is given in the table below.

Dress Sizes

UK	8	10	12	14	16	18
US	6	8	10	12	14	16

Women's Shoes

UK	5	5.5	6	6.5	7
US	6	6.5	7	7.5	8

Men's Shoes

UK	7	7.5	8.5	9.5	10.5	11
US	8	8.5	9.5	10.5	11.5	12

Complaints

New Orleans is well equipped to deal with customer complaints. At a hotel, shop or restaurant make your complaint calmly to the manager.

Any complaints about taxis should be put to the Taxicab Bureau at City Hall, 1300

Perdido Street ☎ 565-6272, and those about public transport to the Regional Transit Authority, 6700 Plaza Drive, ☎ 248-3795.

If you find yourself in a difficult situation, the police and the tourist offices may be able to help.
(*see* **Tourist Information Offices**).

Consulates *

Embassies and consulates can be found at the following addresses:
British Consulate
321 St Charles Avenue,
New Orleans, LA 70130
☎ 524-4180.

Australian Embassy
1601 Massachusetts Avenue, NW, Washington, DC 20036-2273
☎ (202) 797-3000.

Canadian Embassy
501 Pennsylvania Ave NW,
Washington, DC 20001
☎ (202) 682-1740.

Irish Embassy
2234 Massachusetts Ave NW,
Washington, DC 20008
☎ (202) 462-3939.

New Zealand Embassy
37 Observatory Circle NW,
Washington, DC 20008
☎ (202) 328-4800.

Crime

As in many major cities, mugging is a problem. Armstrong Park and certain cemeteries are particularly targeted by muggers and are best avoided at night and when alone. Pickpockets are also rife in the thronging carnival crowds. A few precautions are recommended to reduce the likelihood of becoming a victim:
- Try not to look too obviously like a tourist.
- Don't flash money around.
- Stick to busy tourist areas, especially at night-time; find out which places or areas should be avoided.
- Convention delegates should not wear their identification badges out on the street.
- If confronted by a mugger, the best thing is to hand over whatever is being demanded; keep a small wad of notes handy as a precaution, and this might be sufficient to satisfy the mugger.
- Keep valuables locked in your hotel safe.
- Keep your car locked at all times, and never leave any valuables in it.
- Never open your hotel door to anyone if you are suspicious.

If your passport is stolen,

report it immediately to the nearest consulate. Keep travelers' checks (cheques) separate from the list of their numbers, and in the event of theft report their loss on the telephone number supplied.

Currency *see* **Money**

Customs and Entry Regulations *see* **Arriving**

Disabled Visitors

The US provides exceptional facilities for the disabled, thanks to the 1990 Americans with Disabilities Act. Most public transportation is equipped to take wheelchairs, and attendants accompanying disabled people can often travel free.

All public buildings must, by law, be wheelchair accessible and provide suitable toilet facilities (although historic buildings are exempt), and most street corners slope for easy access. Public telephones are easy to reach, and there are special stalls in public lavatories, Braille indicators in elevators, and an increasing number of reserved parking places.

Popular attractions generally have handicapped facilities, and efforts are made to provide necessary comforts.

Tourist offices provide relevant information for disabled visitors (*see* **Tourist Information Offices**).

Larger hotels have specially designed hotel rooms which should be requested in advance, and the major car rental companies provide cars with hand controls at no extra cost, although these are limited and early reservation is advised.

The Advocacy Center for the Elderly and Disabled, 225 Baronne St, Suite 2112, New Orleans, LA 70112, ☎ **522-2337**, provides a useful guide to French Quarter leisure and entertainment venues accessible to wheelchair users, called *Rolling by the River*. *New Orleans Lodging*, also con-

New Orleans policeman.

taining access advice for disabled people, can be obtained from The New Orleans Metropolitan Convention and Visitors Bureau Inc., 1520 Sugar Bowl Drive, New Orleans, LA 70112, ☎ **566-5011**.

Driving *

Driving in the US is on the right-hand side. Foreign nationals may drive in the US on their own driving license, and fuel is cheap. Speed limits are as follows: 15mph (24kph) in school zones, 30mph (48kph) in business and residential areas, and 55-70mph (88-104kph) on the highways. You are advised to carefully watch the posted speed limits.

Remember that everyone in the car must wear a seat belt. You should pay particular attention when driving in Bayou country, where wildlife wanders freely in the road.

Even among New Orleans residents of the human variety, the rules of the road are loosely followed. Lane discipline is generally lax, as is signaling. It is also common practice to speed up for yellow lights.

Be careful where you park. There are complicated rules regarding where you can and cannot leave your car. If you

Be prepared for alligators in the road.

park within 20ft (7m) of a street-crossing or corner, or a traffic sign, or within 15ft (4.5m) of a fire hydrant your car is liable to be towed away. Pay careful attention to No Parking signs. If you suspect your car has been towed, contact the Claiborne Auto Pound, ☎ **565-7450**. To have your car returned to you will cost $75 plus an additional fine. If you feel that your car

was been towed away unfairly, it is a good idea to take a photograph of the place where your car was parked, as you can use this as evidence in traffic court, and you may well have your fine reimbursed. To avoid these problems, look for a parking lot (car park) or designated meter parking, or, particularly if you are exploring the busy French Quarter, leave your car in the hotel garage.
See also **Car Rental** and **Accidents and Breakdowns**

Dry Cleaning *see* Laundry

Electric Current *
All personal appliances run on 110-115 volts AC, and most sockets are designed to take flat two-pronged plugs. Foreign visitors will need an adaptor for their appliances, which may be bought from electrical goods stores or borrowed from the front desk of large hotels. Appliances rated for other voltages will need a transformer.

Embassies *see* Consulates

Emergencies
Simply dial **911** in an emergency, and the appropriate emergency service will be summoned quickly. Try to give accurate directions, including

hotel name, street name and nearest intersection if you can. Special telephone boxes have been installed on interstate highways at a quarter to half a mile apart, and from one of these you can call for help without dialling **911**. In certain cases, the consulate might help.
See also **Health**

Excursions
The best way to explore the French Quarter is, without doubt, on foot. New Orleans traffic reaches its most haphazard here, where out-of-town drivers mill around, bemused by the confusing street signs, and the lack of traffic lights. Besides, there are so many curiosities and partially hidden beauties to be discovered here that any visit should be leisurely. The grid-layout of the quarter makes it fairly easy for pedestrians to find their way about.

When visiting the Garden District it is also quite wise to leave the car behind. Other areas of the city and out-of-town districts do really call for some method of transportation and are best visited by car for safety reasons.

There are numerous organized tours, which are always a good idea when exploring an area for the first time and for areas where crime is more of a problem. For details contact the tourist offices (*see* **Crime** and **Tourist Information Offices**).

Health *

Travel insurance is essential for foreign visitors to the US, because there is no national health system to provide for medical needs, and private healthcare is very expensive. Travel agents and tour companies will recommend a suitable policy, and this should include at least $1 000 000 for medical expenses.

Should you have a serious accident during your stay, you will be cared for first and asked to pay later. For non-emergencies, look under 'Physicians and Surgeons' or 'Clinics' in the Yellow Pages, but keep all receipts and documentation so that you can claim back any sums you pay out.

Walk-in medical and dental clinics are listed in the telephone directories, and for minor problems drugstores have a huge selection of medicines to offer.

If you know in advance that you will be needing medication in the US, ask your doctor to make out a prescription for the composition of your medicine,

not the brand name.

Hours *see* Opening Hours

Information *see* Tourist Information Offices

Language *

English is the main language, although French may be spoken as a first language by some of the more traditional Creoles and Cajuns in out-of-town Louisiana (though it is not likely to be easily understood by those who have studied standard French). The entirely cosmopolitan nature of New Orleans has ensured that the accent is very distinct from the classic Southern drawl. The speech of the average New Orleanian is clipped and animated.

Various dialects are spoken in different areas of town, according to the racial make-up of the area, but there are several words in general usage in New Orleans which are exclusive to the city and its environs.

Here are a few points of New Orleans' language to note: **Banquette** *ban-KET* Sidewalk/ Pavement. (The original paving consisted of raised wooden platforms, hence the use of this French term, meaning 'bench'.)

Bayou *BY-you* The Southern Louisiana swamplands. The term also denotes a marshy stream.

Carnivalingo The language used to describe the many wonders of the carnival.

De Most locals will use *de* instead of 'the'.

Neutral ground Central reservation between two carriageways. (Originates from when the city was divided into Uptown Anglo and Downtown French sections by Canal Street, which became known as 'The Neutral Ground'.)

New Orleans *noo OR-lins / noo OR-ly-uns / NOR-luns / NUH-waw-lins*

Orleans Avenue *or-LEENS*

Vieux Carré *view ca-RAY* British visitors may be confused by the fact that some words commonly used in British English are used in America to denote entirely different things. Below is a list of some American terms you may find useful.

Laundry

There are plenty of coin-operated laundromats and dry-cleaning establishments. Hotels also usually offer these services, albeit at a higher price.

Lost Property

Report any lost items as soon as you realize they are missing. In hotels, check with the front

American English	British English
restroom	*public toilet*
bathroom	*private toilet*
chips	*crisps*
broiled	*grilled*
trailer	*caravan*
do not pass	*no overtaking*
no standing	*no parking or stopping*
pants	*trousers*
to go	*take-away (food)*
turn-out	*lay-by*
purse	*handbag*
line	*queue*
subway	*underground*
drugstore	*chemist*
check	*bill*

desk or hotel security; local telephone directories have the numbers of taxi companies. When reporting something left in a taxi, if possible give the taxi identification number, shown on the dashboard and on the receipt. Anything lost on a bus or streetcar should be reported to the Regional Transit Authority, 6700 Plaza Drive, ☎ **242-2600**. The police should be informed of any lost travel documents.

Try to obtain a police report if you intend to file a claim for valuable items. Lost or stolen travelers' checks (cheques) and credit cards should be reported immediately to the issuing company with a list of numbers, and the police should also be informed.

Maps

Free maps and brochures, as well as bus and subway maps, are provided by the main tourist centers (*see* **Tourist Information Offices**) and chambers of commerce. Car rental companies also provide free maps that will help with general route planning and driving.

A large-scale motoring map is ideal for serious touring outside the city itself, and may be obtained from any bookshop or gas station. If you do go beyond the city limits, note that state and national parks issue maps of scenic drives, hikes and trails on admission.

Medical Care *see* Health

Money *

US currency is based on the decimal system, with 100 cents to the dollar. Dollar bills are all the same size and color – green – so check the denomination carefully: they come in $1, $5, $10, $20, $50 and $100. $2 notes also exist as legal tender although they are no longer printed, and are very rare. Coins are a dollar, half a dollar (50 cents), a quarter (25 cents), a dime (10 cents), a nickel (5 cents) and a penny (1 cent).

Most things are better value than in the UK, even when the pound is weak against the dollar, so unless you are used to spending vacations in the cheapest of places, you will be in for a pleasant surprise.

The safest way to carry large amounts of money is in dollar travelers' checks (cheques), which are widely accepted and exchanged, or by using a credit card. It is useful to carry change and single dollar bills for tipping.

See also **Tipping** and **Banks**

Newspapers

New Orleans used to support several of its own, very competitive, newspapers. Today, however, there is only one, the *Times-Picayune*. Newspapers from around the US and overseas are also available.

Gambit Weekly is a free publication containing details of what's going on in town. The tourist magazines *This Week in New Orleans* and *Where* are both available from hotels and restaurants free of charge. The monthly magazines, *New Orleans* and *Offbeat* are also good sources of entertainment information.

Opening Hours

Drugstores: Opening times are usually the same as shops, but the Walgreens pharmacy (4400 S Claiborne) and the Eckerd pharmacy (3535 Severn Avenue, Metairie) stay open 24 hours.
Stores: 9.00/10am-5.30/6pm, Monday-Saturday. Shopping malls stay open later, as do shops catering particularly to tourists, especially those in the French Quarter (where some bars stay open 24 hours). These often open on Sundays.
Supermarkets: Most New Orleans supermarkets open from 7am-9pm. Some open 24 hours and many open on Sundays.
Museums and Art Galleries: Opening hours vary greatly, so check at the tourist office when planning your visit.
See also **Post Offices** and **Banks**

Police *

American police are generally helpful and obliging when things go wrong. In an emergency you can get a quick response by telephoning **911**. There are three types of police in the US: the City force; the

...ready for the next city tour.

Sheriff, whose domain is outside the city limits; and the Highway Patrol, who deal with traffic accidents and traffic violations beyond the city limits.

Post Offices

The main post office is located at 701 Loyola Avenue. There are others in the French Quarter, 1022 Iberville Street and 610 South Maestri Place. Post offices are generally open from 9am-4.30/5pm, though these times may vary. Stamps may also be bought from machines which can be found at post offices and in hotels and drugstores, as well as in busy public places such as streetcar terminals. The Central Business District is very well supplied with these vending machines. Mail boxes, painted blue, are on street corners, generally about three blocks apart.

Ordinary mail within the US costs 33 cents for a letter weighing up to one ounce. Airmail between the US and Europe takes about a week; postcards cost 50 cents, aerogrammes are 60 cents and letters weighing up to half an ounce are 60 cents. There are strict rules about sending parcels, which must be contained in special packaging sold by the post office and

sealed according to instructions. Prytania Mail Services, 5500 Prytania Street, ☎ 897-0877 offer an alternative packing and shipping service.

Public Holidays

New Year's Day: 1 January
Martin Luther King Jr's Birthday: 3rd Monday in January
Presidents' Day: 3rd Monday in February
Memorial Day: Last Monday in May
Independence Day: 4 July
Labor Day: 1st Monday in September
Columbus Day: 2nd Monday in October
Veterans Day: 11 November
Thanksgiving Day: 4th Thursday in November
Christmas Day: 25 December
On these days, shops, banks and offices are likely to be closed all day, and in some places Good Friday is a half-day holiday.

Public Transport see Transportation

Religion

There are many churches in New Orleans. Catholicism is the predominant faith, with other Christian denominations and religions also well represented. There is a large Jewish population and numerous synagogues. There are also places of worship for various Middle-Eastern and Far-Eastern religions. Ask your hotel concierge for details. The tourist offices and local Chamber of Commerce may also be able to help. *See also* **Tourist Information Offices**

Smoking

Smoking is frowned upon in the US, though not as severely in New Orleans as in health-conscious California. A large proportion of public places are no-smoking zones, and most restaurants have a large no-smoking section.

Stamps *see* **Post Offices**

Taxis *see* **Transportation**

Telephones *

The easiest way to make an overseas call is from a hotel room, and although this is more expensive than using a public telephone, it can save a lot of time and energy. You can also call collect or use your overseas credit card by dialling **0** for the operator. To dial direct from a public telephone, dial **011** plus the country code (UK **44**; Eire **353**; Australia, **61** New Zealand **64**) plus area

A novel mail box captures the unconventional spirit of New Orleans.

code plus telephone number. Make sure that you have a good supply of money in small coins. The lowest rates for international calls to Europe are generally in effect between 6pm and 7am, and the same is true for local and long-distance calls within the US. The rate for local calls will be shown in the telephone booth.

There are more than 100 area codes in the US. The area code for New Orleans is **985**. To call outside your area code, dial **1** plus the area code plus number.

Time Difference

New Orleans is in the Central Standard Time (CST) zone, which is six hours behind Greenwich Mean Time (GMT). Daylight Saving Time lasts from the first Sunday in April when clocks are advanced one hour, until the last Sunday in October.

Tipping *

Tipping is standard practice in the US. The accepted – and expected – rates are 15-20 per cent in restaurants, 15 per cent for taxis, 10-20 per cent for hairdressers and barbers and 10 per cent for bartenders and cocktail servers. Chambermaids should receive $2 for each day of your stay, porters about $1 per bag, and doormen $1 for hailing a taxi.

Toilets

Public toilets are rare in New Orleans. However, many public buildings provide lavatories for the use of the general public. These facilities – known as rest rooms, powder rooms, or men's/women's rooms – are usually well maintained. Restaurants and cafés also have good facilities. In restaurants and theaters, where there is an attendant, a small tip will be expected.

Tourist Information Offices

For general information about your stay in New Orleans visit **The New Orleans Metropolitan Convention and Visitors Bureau Inc.**, based at 1520 Sugar Bowl Drive, New Orleans, LA 70112, ☎ **566-5011**, or see them at the New Orleans International Airport (next to the Customs Desk). **The New Orleans Welcome Center** is in the same building as the **Louisiana State Information Center** at 529 St Ann Street, Jackson Square, ☎ **566-5031**. All these organistions offer a wide range of maps, brochures and guides, plus information on accommodations, seasonal events, eating facilities, places

All dressed for St Patrick's Day.

of interest and sightseeing tours.

Folklorists regard New Orleans and South Louisiana as America's richest region of African cultural retention. In addition, the city's African-Americans boast a distinguished historic legacy. For information with an African-American orientation, contact the Greater New Orleans Black Tourism Network (☎ **800 725-5652, 523-5652**). (All 800 numbers are toll-free within the US.)

For information before you leave home, the United States Travel and Tourism Administration has offices in US embassies and consulates throughout the world.

Tours see **Excursions**

Transportation
The best way to get around the French Quarter (and possibly the Garden District) is on foot. For other areas the buses and streetcars run by the Regional Transit Authority provide a good service. When using the buses, do make sure you have the exact fare as the driver carries no change. Some hotels and stores sell VisiTour Passes. These are travel cards allowing unlimited travel on the street-cars and buses at $5 for one day and $12 for 3 days. Be aware that pickpockets operate on public transport systems.
Taxis are fairly easy to come by. They gather particularly in the areas most frequented by tourists: outside large hotels; theaters; and stations and terminals. There are also several good telephone taxi sevices, such as the United Cab Company (☎ **522-9771**).
Ferries cross the river at various points. They are free to passengers, although some make a charge for cars. The ferry between Canal Street and Algiers is a favorite among residents and visitors alike. The last ferry leaves from the end of Canal Street at 9.30pm and stays in Algiers overnight.
See also **Disabled Visitors** and

Enjoying the crawfish – a great New Orleans moment.

Tourist Information Offices

TV and Radio

Radio stations are plentiful. They generally play a specific genre of music, or specialize in talk shows or continual news. WWOZ, 90.7 FM, airs local music 24 hours a day. There are four nationwide TV networks: ABC, CBS, NBC and Fox. PBS (cultural channel) and cable also offer a burgeoning variety of choices. Very frequent commercial breaks are a feature of most American broadcast media.

Water

New Orleans' drinking water is safe to drink. If you prefer, there is a wide variety of bottled water available.

INDEX

INDEX